Endorsements

A few years ago, a small group of women in our local church was experiencing difficulty connecting with others and staying connected. Outside of sharing Jesus, these women also shared the commonality of broken relationships, sometimes the fractured relationship being due to fleeing abuse. They needed extra care, attention, patience, and every other virtue that describes the love we find in 1 Corinthians 13:4–8. As I asked the Lord for help and provision within His church to care for these women, Denise Renken's face kept popping into my head. Knowing her for over a decade, she was always the woman who would say "yes" to care for the hurting, broken, and hopeless, whether the request came from me or our marriage ministry. When she honored me by sharing her whole story with David present, it all clicked: "Her many sins have been forgiven—as her great love has shown. But whoever has been forgiven little loves little." Denise is marked by the one action that Jesus says marks His disciples: *love.* I'm so excited for you to meet my friend and Jesus's disciple as you work to untangle your past and move toward healing guided by Denise's story, insights from God's Word and the psychological developmental process, and reflection questions in *Triage*.

—**Rob Barry**
Retired Elder, Watermark Community Church, Dallas, TX

Triage is a valuable resource for women who seek release from the life-crippling grip of their negative pasts. In this well-researched and practical how-to book, Denise Renken shares her own raw journey from the darkness of trauma to the sweetness only achieved through God's healing. With honesty and vulnerability, Denise leads the reader to spiritual healing, wholeness, and a fresh relationship with the God who desires her flourishing.

This book is a must-read for anyone wanting to leave the heavy burdens of the past behind and move forward—renewed and restored.

—**Cheryl Schuermann**
Author, *Farmhouse Devotions*

Denise Renken's *Triage* is a powerful story of emotional trauma and the wounds created. This is a journey of healing and forgiveness through the blood of Jesus. Everyone's pain may look different, but the same Jesus provides healing for us all. This book is a must-read!

—**Carla Shelton**
Author, *Conquering the Book Thief*
Radio Podcast, *Monday Manna*

Denise Renken's latest project, *Triage,* explores her past hurts to show readers how to mend their mental and spiritual wounds. Her testimony about God's faithfulness in her life resonates with many of my core beliefs. Her practical activities will help the reader complete the journey to wholeness. Be ready to dig into your spiritual roots to heal from your past.

—**Jennifer Wake**
Author, *Call Signs* and *He Is Jehovah*

Triage is a powerful and courageous story of how God loves us personally and provides for our every need when we submit to Him. The author grew up with neglect and abuse and was launched into a dark world of sin and struggle. But God pursued her. She learned to listen, obey, and finally committed her life to Jesus, where she found freedom and healing. Denise Renken is a beautiful example of how God can heal us and bring joy. I recommend this book for all who carry heavy burdens and have yet to meet their Savior.

—**Kristy Sheridan**
Author, *Third Save*

Triage is an unbelievable true story written with courage, vulnerability, practicality, and wisdom. This is a great text to counsel individuals and married or premarital couples. Denise Renken brings a unique voice and perspective by utilizing the Bible and the best of the social sciences. I am recommending all the missionaries in our organization read, study, and inwardly digest *Triage*.

—**Larry Merino, PhD**
Pastor of Missional Discipleship, Holy Cross Lutheran Church
President and Founder, Gospel to the Gypsies, Inc., Fort Wayne, IN

TRIAGE

HEALING
MENTAL
AND
SPIRITUAL
ROOTS

Denise Renken

©2025 by Denise Renken. All rights reserved.

Published by Redemption Press, 1602 Cole Street, Enumclaw, WA 98022, (360) 226-3488.

Redemption Press is honored to present this title in partnership with the author. The views expressed or implied in this work are those of the author. Redemption Press provides our imprint seal representing design excellence, creative content, and high-quality production.

Noncommercial interests may reproduce portions of this book without express written permission of the author, provided the text does not exceed five hundred words. When reproducing text from this book, include the following credit line: "Triage by Denise Renken, used by permission."

Commercial interests: no part of this publication may be reproduced in any form, stored in a retrieval system, or transmitted in any form by any means—electronic, photocopy, recording, or otherwise—without prior written permission of the publisher/author, except as provided by United States of America copyright law.

Unless otherwise noted, all Scripture quotations are taken from the Holy Bible, English Standard Version® (ESV). Copyright ® 2001 Crossway. Used by permission. All rights reserved.

ISBN: 978-1-64645-913-1 (Paperback)
ISBN: 978-1-64645-914-8 (eBook)
Library of Congress Catalog Card Number: 2025905024.

This book is dedicated to all women.

You are my beloved sisters.

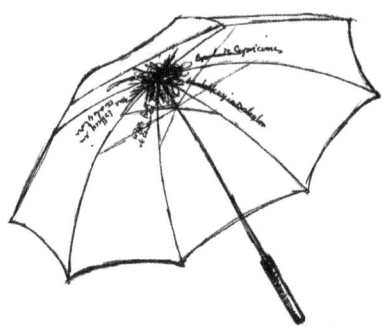

Acknowledgments

To David, my husband and champion. Through forty-seven years of highs and lows, you were the one who asked, "How can I help?" You lived through the difficulty of penning this book, the tug on my soul for women's hearts, and my passion to serve them. Through stressful moments and joyous moments, support thrived. Thank you.

To the thousands of women who heard my testimony, you pressed me to *tell all.* My love for you set this book in motion.

Cheryl Schuermann, you guided me through this foreign world called publishing and believed in this project from the beginning. We come from such different worlds yet quickly became sisters.

To my family, your extension of grace reflects a heart for God. What a precious gift to me.

To my daily prayer warriors, Amie, Laura, and Michelle, you drew swords on the battlefield to challenge Satan's internal dialogue with me. God bless you.

To my friends, who I affectionately call "The page 54 and 55 Word Weavers International critique group," y'all deserve a Purple Heart. You encouraged, corrected, shed tears, and asked, "Where's the popcorn for this movie?" Thank you for embracing my journey.

To my community group, y'all took one for the team. You listened to my fears and frustrations and prayed for me. Thank you.

To Redemption Press, thank you for your support from start to finish and then beyond.

Contents

Introduction: How to Get the Most Out of This Book	1
Section I: Evaluate the Influence of Past Years	9
Chapter 1: Why Do I Struggle with Trust?	11
Chapter 2: What Is the Source of Shame and Self-Doubt?	17
Chapter 3: Will I Always Carry This Guilt?	27
Chapter 4: Why Do I Feel Inferior?	41
Chapter 5: Who Am I? Finding My Identity	61
Section II: Adulthood	77
Chapter 6: What Drives the Desire to Isolate?	79
Chapter 7: Selling Ourselves	89
Section III: New Beginnings	99
Chapter 8: Does God Care?	101
Chapter 9: Marriage, Divorce, Marriage	115
Section IV: The Path to Healing	121
Chapter 10: God Draws Us to Him	123
Chapter 11: Going Home	139
Section V: Restoration	154
Chapter 12: Triage Heart Repair	155
Chapter 13: Molded by the Master's Hands	171
Chapter 14: A Note from David	183
Chapter 15: Conflict Resolution	195
Chapter 16: What Satan Meant for Evil, God Uses for Good	203
Appendix: Finding a Mentor	207
Notes	211
About the Author	213

Triage

Triage, a French word meaning "to sort," was initially used to sort agricultural products by quality. Its use later evolved to the medical field, prioritizing casualties at three levels of needed treatment.

As it pertains to this book, "triage" sorts mental and spiritual wounds in search of root causes. One by one, they are left on the throne of God for His healing.

Introduction
How to Get the Most Out of This Book

> As for you, you meant evil against me, but God meant
> it for good, to bring it about that many people
> should be kept alive, as they are today.
> —Genesis 50:20

> The intuitive withdrawal into a fetal position
> braced me for the inevitable—the pull of the trigger.
> —Denise Renken

Each day presents a set of life choices, some trivial, others life-altering. The method we use to make our determinations is a product of past experiences and current spiritual health. Both hold power. But how do we release the life-crippling grip of our negative experiences so we can heal? It is God who unleashes His power to mend our hearts and minds—not for a day or a year, but forever. Any damage inflicted upon us by individuals and ourselves falls to the ground in submission before Him. Only then do we rise in triumph.

I invite you to walk with me through a process to help you better understand yourself and the power of God to mend wounds. I have many wounds you may or may not have experienced, including sexual abuse, poverty, and a violent, heroin-addicted father. As I revisit my date rape, homelessness, prostitution, and abortion, my memories will assist in springboarding the identification and analysis of *your* wounds. Recognizing wounds creates a connection to specific prayer and God's hand of redemption. Life's possibilities change when we trust God.

It has been my privilege to mentor women for over thirty-five years. Ladies say, "I don't trust, I don't know, I don't believe God can restore my heart." I respond, "There has never been anyone, not Mary, Ruth, or Esther, who has been loved more than you. The Holy Bible is your guidepost to the truth: God loves you and heals."

Triage is my desire to embrace a world of women bound by past and current events. Satan encourages the world to toss struggling lives, relationships, and marriages into the garbage. He generates internal dialogues telling us nothing will ever change, we don't matter, and we deserve a chaotic life. I cannot change your current circumstances, but I'm offering a path to change how you make future decisions, to make choices with the discernment of God. Are you weary of chasing the world's solutions? Are you ready to ask God, "What is Your plan?" May God's peace gather you up to Him so you can seek His path for recovery from the hurts this world has inflicted upon you. God can create a new woman with a heart prepared for healthy relationships if you will let Him.

Where Did I Begin?

When the time arrives to sort out your life, it forces the question, "Where do I begin?" I wasn't ready to share my past, not even with a professional counselor, nor could I afford it.

I needed to narrow my focus on the damage the events caused, the root causes. But a thick, impenetrable fog surrounded me. Thoughts of escape were met with the reminder of the shackles binding me to past regrets. My mind raced, heart pounded. The entangled mountain of disastrous life decisions seemed overwhelming. I recognized the road signs in front of me: *Turn Now. Decide Now.* I didn't know what it meant to be a daughter of God, but He met me with His provision of peace and clarity for what lay ahead. I urge you to please step into His arms. He will meet you, take your hand, and guide you.

I needed a simple solution, but my search to locate "simple" took place in the days before computers or the internet. I spent exhaustive days in the library, searching for my easy, which led to Erik Erikson's books. Erikson's process for healing was ideal for several reasons. It was straightforward and respected worldwide, and did I mention *simple*? His methodology led me to discover that the emotional damage I was carrying need only be placed at the throne of God. *Triage* marries the mental and spiritual healing of root causes, and I will show you step-by-step in each section.

How Did I Discover What Needed to Be Healed?

Erikson's background and his methodology help people to identify life wounds. A winner of the Pulitzer Prize for his structure of *life stages*, Erik H. Erikson was a renowned German psychologist. He is best known for developing the framework used to analyze critical events in our lives, mapping our lives into eight stages. These stages include psychological and social needs from birth to death, making it easier to dissect significant patterns. Perhaps you have heard the term "formative years" when discussing child development. It was Erikson who created the "Formative Years" concept. The first four stages of our lives comprise these years.

Per Erikson, each stage faces a crisis. These crises do not represent anything negative, but they are hurdles to mental growth for us to overcome. Crises shape our physical and psychological development and our success in life. The way the crisis is handled determines our characteristics and strengths and shapes our personality. Think of a baby. Gaining the ability to roll over will lead to crawling, which will lead to walking and then running. The first crisis is whether the child will roll over. If she rolls over, she is better equipped for the next stage and its crisis. Each stage builds on the successes and failures of the previous stage. Running will prove difficult if she has not learned to walk.

A layman's understanding of what should have been achieved during each stage is presented in this book.

I have structured each chapter as follows:

My story. Beginning at birth and continuing in chronological order, I will share my past experiences within each of Erikson's stages. The impact of violence, mental abuse, sexual abuse, abandonment, date rape, abortion, prostitution, marriages, divorces, my alcoholic/heroin-addicted father, and more are poured out. Since God holds the power to redeem and restore, my hope is that my life wounds can be used to better assist you in understanding *your* hurts. I recognize people have experienced differing levels of harm. This book addresses experiences similar to mine or those involving less trauma.

Erikson's life stages, by age group, and the crisis in each stage. What should we achieve (the crisis) versus the residual damage if achievement falls short? We already know that past harms have created current issues. Erikson provides a more thorough understanding of the damage generated, providing a path for God's healing.

Reflection Sections. Sprinkled throughout the chapters, I have written some reflections about what God was doing in my life or things I noticed or learned about His character. On your own journey, you might want to journal your own reflections about God's intervention in your life.

Triage Questions. In chapters one through eight, I've included questions for you to answer to help you process your stages.

Closing Triage Prayer. Each chapter ends with a Triage Prayer to guide your thoughts and prayers.

Before you begin, I also want to provide a few guidelines to help you with healing your mental and spiritual roots:

- Approach your mental and spiritual restoration with a mindset of grace for yourself and others. Your parents may have been great, but there may have been hurts created in your formative years. You will examine big and small wounds inflicted on you. This requires a God-centered heart, one empty of the desire to seek revenge or conflict, hold resentment, or blame. A humbled heart requests God's mercy and restorative hands.

- Dissecting the past is not limited to traumatic events. I also want you to seek out and find the sweet times of God's presence.

- As we navigate this journey together, we will pray to transfer the weight of your burdens to God's shoulders. Allow Him to carry the wounds of your heart.

TRIAGE

- Although not essential, you may find it helpful to have a friend walk this process with you. The appendix contains helpful information on mentoring. Jesus and I navigated my wounds, just the two of us, for many years. When the time came to widen my circle of help, I sought a Christian psychologist. I openly shared things with him that I feared would change how my friends saw me. There are alternative resources to paid counseling, which I'll share within the appropriate chapter.

- I encourage you to spend this season praying for yourself, just you. It will strengthen your relationship with God and provide healing to your soul. God is aware of all the other people in need of prayer. Trust the Holy Spirit to lift those folks to God. Instead, pray for your needs, desires, restoration, and peace. Permit yourself to spend a season with only you and God.

- As I unpack my formative years as an example for you, it's your turn to create a list of impactful events from *your* formative years. This list should include the offender, the offense, and, most importantly, the *damage* caused by the event. This will be clarified as you move through the book. Remember, don't limit this inventory to the negative. Find the sweet moments.

Ladies, you are precious to God, created in His image. Your mental and spiritual health matter to Him. I pray comfort and healing to your soul and that you feel His presence and my love as you move forward. I'm so proud of you.

Section I

Evaluate the Influence of Past Years

Chapter 1
Why Do I Struggle with Trust?

Stage One: Birth to Eighteen Months

The ability to trust ourselves and others is formed in the first eighteen months of life. I find this concept startling. However, when I examined my own trust issues, it confirmed the impact this period had on my life. We spend our future years either repairing the damage incurred during a stage or exacerbating the issues. When you review your stages, approach them knowing that most things matter. You'll want to think about things like socioeconomic impact, family structure, extended relationships, strangers, culture, faith, and so forth.

For my stage one, I relied mostly on others' memories. Mama waited tables at the local burger restaurant. Serving was the most a young woman might aspire to unless your family could afford nursing, teaching, or secretarial school—careers that occupied the top rung for women in the 1940s and 1950s.

Mama and Daddy embraced the fun-loving party lifestyle. A whirlwind courtship led to marriage; they were eighteen and twenty.

My older sister Marilyn was three when I came along in 1954. My sister Judy's birth followed four years after me in 1958. Three East Texas girls born into chaos.

Good times didn't last. The home became riddled with alcoholism and violence. Daddy came from a family of blackout drunks, where frequent visits by the sheriff to restore peace represented his view of normal.

His alcohol addiction progressed to heroin while serving as a Marine in the Korean Conflict (War). Where there is substance abuse, violence soon follows. While he never struck me or my sisters, he used fists on my mother, hurling her against walls. They often screamed at one another, and her tears became a regular occurrence.

This home, bred of *fear*, *instability*, and *anxiety*, would lead to my *extreme avoidance of conflict* and *strict obedience to any perceived authority*. And, to this day, a lingering *struggle with trust*.

Note that the events were violence and substance abuse related. Other events pertaining to my daddy will be shared later. Examples of the damage caused by the events are italicized in the previous paragraph. You can use this as a guideline to create your list.

Exploring Erikson's Stage One
The Crisis: Trust vs. Mistrust

As infants, we evaluate our ability to rely on our caregiver for the essential needs of food, comfort, safety, and positive environmental stimulus, including peace in the home. Parenting mistakes will happen. If mistakes are the exception, we will distinguish the difference. Lifelong patterns form. Will we trust the concept of relationships, trust others, and trust ourselves?

The establishment of trust is "the cornerstone of a vital personality"[1] [and the framework of trust] "forms the basis in the child for a sense of identity which will later combine a sense of being 'all right,' of being oneself."[2]

Reflection

Although I continue to struggle with trust, God mended the crippling impact of my stage one. In the past, I avoided relationships, and socializing with others was painfully awkward. Now, I trust in God and His plan for my life, which frees me to trust people.

As children, we blindly offer our confidence. As adults, we learn to adjust expectations. I'm trustworthy. Or am I? Even I can be selfish, want my way, and be so shocked by a situation that I lean on my own understanding before asking God. But God is good, pure; He is holy. My faith is in Him. He will provide the discernment needed to evaluate those around me for trustworthiness.

Breaches in trust need to be viewed through God's lens. He tells us to guard our hearts (Proverbs 4:23). Apologies received or extended do not necessarily restore confidence; trust must be earned, but not with an adversarial approach or vindictiveness. Hostility does not reflect the heart of God. Forgiveness can be extended, but trust takes time.

Triage Questions

You may never receive acknowledgment or apologies for past harm. I am sorry for everything done to you, care not given you, love withheld, and the weight of carrying the pain. I'm sorry for how the past has colored your decisions and how you processed your worth. If deep wounds are leading to dark thoughts of suicide, seek professional assistance now. God created your life and breathed it into your lungs. He wants you rejuvenated, as do I.

If you don't get anything else from my story, know this: The source of our internal dialogue is either from God or Satan. It's as simple as that. Satan tells you, "You don't matter." God says, "You are Mine, loved and valued; come to Me." Close your eyes, sit quietly, and feel His arms wrap around you.

TRIAGE

1. Did you leave stage one with your ability to trust?

    a. If so, how is trust exhibited in your closest relationships?

    b. If not, how does the lack of trust continue to limit your relationships?

2. Do you trust God?

    a. If yes, what events have occurred in your life to bring you to this place of trust?

    b. If not, try to understand the root cause. For me, the lack of trust in an earthly father blocked my recognition of a good, heavenly Father for many years. I could not trust the concept of a loving father who wanted the best for me. When I prayed for the courage to love and trust God, He *immediately* began my sweet redemption.

Triage Prayer

Father, please remove the remnants of distrust. Grant us wisdom to discern trustworthiness through Your lens and not ours. Dismantle our emotional walls and tenderly guide our hearts to the other side. Help us know we only need to trust You to carry us through the valleys of life.

We yearn for the peace and lasting joy only found with You. Thank You for the privilege of calling You Father.

In Jesus's name, Amen

Chapter 2
What Is the Source of Shame and Self-Doubt?

Stage Two: Eighteen Months to Three Years

Although he never beat us, Daddy would, on occasion, play horrid psychological games; he would hide us from Mama in deserted, lifeless places. When I was three, the deep concrete culvert where he deposited Marilyn and me became a massive playground. We investigated its entirety with fascination. Climbing the steep and slippery sides proved fruitless. Looking back, I choose to believe rain was not in the forecast. What did Marilyn think and feel? Daddy bent down, whispering something to her before turning to leave. Did she feel responsible for me? I suspect she did. Oldest children so often step into part-time parental roles. It seemed like an eternity in the culvert before his return.

On another occasion, he abandoned us half a mile from my maternal grandparents' home (Papaw and Nannie). It was a wintery night when Daddy placed us in a ditch beside the one-lane country road. Disoriented, wearing nothing but our panties, we were gripped by fear. Memories of the pitch-black night and the dampness of the tall overgrowth of weeds remain. Our embraces brought little comfort as we clung together for assurance and warmth.

Daddy phoned Papaw, who came to retrieve us from the dark. Sounds of sobbing little girls revealed our location as Papaw drove the road in search of us. Our tear-stained faces stared into the eyes of our Papaw. After scooping us into his arms, he wrapped us in blankets and tenderly placed us into the not-yet-warm car.

Daddy's hands represented anger and fear, Papaw's offered love and care. This moment with Papaw forged an unshakable bond between us. His calm demeanor eliminated additional emotion in a despondent and desperate moment. I loved my Papaw—he was my hero. The warmth and safety radiated within their home gave us a welcome sigh of relief. I don't have any knowledge of the adult conversations and decisions made in the aftermath.

Reflection

Dumped into the wet ditch, shivering in the cold, God protected us from harm—from snakes and other predators.

The eyes of the Lord are in every place, keeping watch on the evil and the good.
(Proverbs 15:3)

TRIAGE

The contrast in behavior between Daddy and Papaw was a gift from God. Comparisons can often show us the differences in how God views our value versus a world requiring us to earn scraps of value from its table of perceived worthiness.

Exploring Erikson's Stage Two
The Crisis: Autonomy vs. Shame and Doubt

Autonomy, self-governing, is the ability to make good life decisions. In this stage, we begin to distance ourselves from our caregivers. Seeking independence, we release the grip on the hand once held and take those first steps. Muscle development allows toilet training to take place, and we begin to sense potential control of our decisions, "retaining or releasing" the bowels and bladder.

"This whole stage, then, becomes a battle for autonomy."[1] Whereas shaming leads to doubt, consistent boundaries concerning expectations remain necessary. I'm not suggesting children should be allowed to throw tantrums, soil themselves, or scream demands. But telling toddlers they are bad or using harsh treatment is not the solution. God created us to respond to encouragement, value, and respect. All these things signal love. We become well-functioning adults as a result of being well-loved children.

If parents give "too rigid or early training," she loses part of her "free will."[2] "This stage, therefore, becomes decisive for the ratio between loving good will and hateful self-insistence, between co-operation and willfulness, and between self-expression and compulsive self-restraint or meek compliance."[3]

A toddler clearly understands the word "no" and begins to use it. Their likes and dislikes begin to form. Is the home operated as a dictatorship with no grace for errors? The parent may want toilet training accomplished by a particular date, want control of nap time, or be intolerant of the messes children create. Are parental unmet goals managed well?

If not, "later attempts in adult life will lead to govern[ing] by the letter, rather than by the spirit."[4]

Domination of the child puts later years at risk of turning from God or toward harsh religious legalism versus a relationship with Jesus.

Triage Questions

1. Did this stage give you confidence to approach new tasks and opportunities? Or are you fearful of trying new things?

2. We all fail. How do you manage failures? Are you defeated or willing to try again?

3. Are there secrets in need of sharing with a trusted friend? Who can you share them with, and are you ready to do this?

Reflection

While living with Mama and Daddy, I exited this stage with shame and doubt rather than autonomy. The violence, chaos, and abandonment continued to drive home the message: trust no one. The formation of independent thought lacked fostering. Failure was a common feeling. Secrets were the norm. We were told, "Don't tell anyone what Daddy did."

God has since pressed into my heart that secrets give Satan power. When we share them with other believers, it releases the power of the secret. The healing ability of Jesus takes over. Residual feelings of shame and doubt can allow us to be more easily manipulated by predators.

> *Therefore, confess your sins to one another and*
> *pray for one another,*
> *that you may be healed.*
> *(James 5:16)*

TRIAGE

Why Reading the Bible Is So Important

Reading the Bible is vitally important to our mental and spiritual health. The Bible provides a window into the mind and heart of God and how much He truly loves and values us. I wrote a blog post in 2023 that I hope encourages you. Many women struggle with daily reading. You are not a failure in your walk with God.

In a Rut?

Self-exam time. I've been known to allow busyness to push my Bible time aside. There have been extended periods when I consistently read, meditated, and journaled my thoughts. Yet, once again, I would get off track. As if knocked off the road into a ditch, a rut.

I'm a creature of habit, a proactive planner. Preparation brings order to my life and is comforting. So why did this proactive planner get knocked into a rut? Was there a road sign, "Warning, Rut Ahead?" How had I missed the cue?

First, a rut is precisely where Satan wants us. There, he can keep us from being our best. He wins when we're stuck in a world without our Bible. We become doubtful about God's plan for us and make excuses, typically, "I'm too busy." Satan triggers our internal dialogue, telling us we're unqualified to do whatever current God-mission awaits us. He points out a new wrinkle on our forehead. We're getting old. He says everyone, except us, is taking a marvelous trip. Or he feeds our stress by convincing us to add one more thing to the to-do list.

Second, we can fall into a rut when major projects arise. Moving, that's a big one. It takes such effort mentally and physically and stretches over weeks or months. That's long enough to get the wheels bogged. Deaths, births, illness, new jobs, and getting the kiddos back in school all can knock us off the road.

Ladies, we're clever. We know the value of balancing physical, mental, and spiritual to run life well. I am a better daughter of God when I tend to all three. What I pour into my marriage, family, and precious friends is more fruitful when I manage all three. But in the moments of life's obstacles, I have been known to fall into a rut. If we acknowledge what is at risk, we can better manage the landslides of life so we don't get tossed into a ditch. I now see the early warning signs and avoid them. I'm more *aware* of how busy seasons can impact my time with God; awareness makes it easier to stay on the path.

God's Word should be as important as the air we breathe. Why would we go another day without it? If you don't own a Bible, I recommend a Study Bible. A Study Bible combines the Bible and a theologian's comments about each passage. I own many Bible translations by various commentators. John MacArthur's Study Bible was my first and continues to be a favorite. It is less intimidating when a good commentator holds your hand. God speaks to us through His Word and the Holy Spirit. We communicate with Him in prayer. Healthy relationships are never one-sided. When funds are lacking, I put a new Bible on my birthday, Mother's Day, and Christmas wish lists. They make treasured gifts.

I do not participate in "read the Bible in a year" marathons. Some love to speed read; I prefer a stroll. My stroll takes five years from start to finish. Choose your speed; don't worry about other people.

Some love to journal. It is a forced event for me. I jot my thoughts and prayers after reading a section. I always benefit from journaling, yet it continues to be a struggle.

The important questions: Are you in a rut? What is your next step to climb out of the rut?

Triage Prayer

Father, Satan wants us to be plagued by shame and doubt. It cripples our lives, robs us of our joy and peace. You see our value. You perfectly created us for Your plan. Place a yearning in our souls to read the Bible. Allow its encouragement and wisdom to bathe us in peace.

In Jesus's name, Amen

Chapter 3
Will I Always Carry This Guilt?

Stage Three: Three to Five

Perhaps because I resembled him, I was Daddy's favorite. As a result, he regularly took me to bars in the midmorning. These were sleazy bars occupied by drunks at that time of day.

At high speed, we flew down the two-lane highway connecting our backwoods home to the surrounding small towns. The wind coming through the open windows energized me. Music played on the radio. In 1957, seat belts didn't exist. One day, in his hurry to get to the bar, he failed to close the rear car door, and I tumbled out of the back seat, bouncing from the roadside gravel into the weeds. At some point, Daddy realized what happened and returned to find me.

Scrapes and open wounds from the gravel required minor attention. The real damage manifested itself as anxiety, along with feelings of fear and abandonment. As I think back on the trips to the alcoholic-ridden places, filled with men drinking excessively, I do not recall them abusing me.

Reflection

If something happened to me in one of those horrid bars, God has blocked it from my memory, and I thank Him.

> *The Lord is my rock and my fortress and*
> *my deliverer, my God, my rock, in whom*
> *I take refuge, my shield, and the horn*
> *of my salvation, my stronghold.*
> *(Psalm 18:2)*

Our house was little more than an unpainted shack along a dusty road surrounded by pastures for cattle and fields of tall grass. We rented our house from one of the nearby farmers. Others would have considered us poor, but children don't understand economic demographics. In my last family memory, Daddy was chasing a rat with a broom held high. Marilyn, Mama, and I stood on the kitchen table. Mama screamed as Daddy ran around the table with the bare light bulb above us swinging wildly. The entire scene was hysterically funny to Marilyn and me.

Later that night, drunk again, Daddy got on the neighbor's tractor and plowed up half of the neighbor's field, then came home and beat Mama. Earlier in the day, eight-year-old Marilyn, realizing alcohol was responsible for the fighting and violence, had poured it out while Daddy was gone. When he returned, believing Mama was responsible, his anger erupted.

Poor Marilyn. She trembled and wept in the small bed we shared on the screened-in back porch. In a failed attempt to block the sounds of his rage and Mama's screams, we pressed tiny hands over our ears, tears streaming. The sheriff's arrival and the landlord's angry verbal eviction notice are in my memory, but I have no other recollection of the event.

The severity of the beating was the catalyst for Mama to seek help. Papaw, determined to get us far away from Daddy, contacted his sister in California. He purchased train tickets and helped gather our meager belongings. At the station, he slipped Mama a little pocket money. In May 1959, we left Daddy. Once there, we lived with my great-aunt. The Spirit of God glowed on her face as she opened her home to us. I am uncertain of the long-term plan, but we relished the adventure.

Without our knowledge, Daddy discovered where we had gone and soon followed. My aunt opened the front door in response to his pounding fists. I saw him on the porch, but I never noticed the gun. The following morning, eavesdropping around the corner, I listened to whispers at the kitchen table. They spoke of Daddy threatening to kill Mama, resulting in a call to the police. Daddy was not prosecuted, but it was the last time I saw him.

When it came time for me to process my forgiveness for the damage he caused, I discovered he had lived the remainder of his days on the West Coast. He was buried in a military cemetery. He served his country, and I am glad he is honored in that place. My forgiveness, which I'll tell more about later, removed the shackles of harm linked to him.

The next week, Papaw wired funds for our return to Texas. He kept a shotgun nearby for trouble daring to follow us. Oh my, what fun on the train. Mama was busy with baby Judy. Marilyn and I ran from train car to train car as if no one had ever taught us any better. What a wonderful gift to be a kid for a while.

Once we settled back in Texas, we moved into public housing. Mama immediately filed for divorce and secured a job at a local café. Public housing was different in the 1950s. You stayed briefly to transition and get back on your feet. The little apartments in East Texas were all one-story fourplexes.

Mama worked hard hours at the café, quickly moving from server to manager. Arrangements were made with a neighbor for our daily care. Her gray hair stretched to the floor before being piled on her head each morning. Marilyn and I would sit mesmerized as we watched her hair spiral upward.

The smell of freshly baked biscuits drew us toward the kitchen. She always made enough for us and the birds we fed outside her back door. We watched, with childish delight, from the kitchen window as they danced around, grabbing the biscuit crumbs.

Day by day, Mama began experiencing frequent headaches. These quickly escalated in severity, becoming unbearable. Doctors discovered a mass in her brain. A biopsy indicated no cancer. The family was informed that the mass was probably a result of repeated blows to the head. Surgery spared her life, but the removal of the mass left significant brain damage. From the age of twenty-seven, she would continue to use a wheelchair until her premature death at the age of fifty-nine.

We moved in with Papaw and Nannie. They lived in a simple white house with green trim, situated off the state highway, down a dusty Texas country road. Years before, Papaw had bought the land and moved a rundown house onto the ten-acre property. Through the years, he made repairs. The little house was in sound condition when we assumed residence.

Red oaks ran down both sides of the house, with a two-acre garden to the west side beyond the oaks. Behind the house stood clotheslines, three barns in varying stages of decline, a trellis for grapevines, and pens for rabbits. Past the oaks on the east side of the house, the two acres of grassy area served as a playground. Beyond the grassy area were Mr. Green's pastures for his cattle, stock ponds, and more trees. All provided a marvelous place for children to explore.

To the south, beyond the barns, rested more pastureland and, in the distance, dense woods. Beyond the woods was the Black community, set apart by a system beyond the understanding of a young child, still innocent of the structuring of such horrid, manufactured rules. Back on the main highway, a gas station was on one side and a small country store on the other. Another thirty miles east led to the outskirts of Texarkana, TX. All of this became my new home.

Mama's brain impairment impacted the control of her motor skills. She could not feed herself or walk. I watched as she learned to feed herself again. The process frightened my five-year-old mind. She barely resembled the woman I called Mama. She learned to use a fork or spoon but never regained the ability to use a knife and fork together.

Her daily rehab exercises were a curiosity to me. Lying on the bed, she would shakily raise one leg into the air, lower it, and then raise the other. Eventually, she gained the ability to lift herself from the wheelchair. Leaning forward, she clung to the wall for security and took slow, deliberate, jerky steps to move short distances—all accomplished while holding on to the wall. This mobility allowed her to take care of her basic personal needs. Life with Mama would never be the same.

Papaw and Nannie still had two of their eight children at home (teens) and Nannie's mother (my great-grandmother, Granny). They struggled to manage this new life with an invalid daughter and three young grandchildren. One-year-old Judy was sent to live with Mama's oldest sister and her family. I would only see Judy at rare family get-togethers. For all intents and purposes, I lost my baby sister and felt her absence during the days and years ahead. The lack of bonding time created an emptiness in my heart. I felt like a part of me had splintered away.

Reflection

As I reconciled with God, He created my passion for women who are hurting. My sisters in Christ have filled the emptiness created by the loss of loved ones.

TRIAGE

For in him all the fullness of God was pleased to dwell,
and through him to reconcile to himself all things,
whether on earth or in heaven, making peace
by the blood of his cross.
(Colossians 1:19–20)

Scattered memories of my brief time with Granny resurface from time to time. Her rocking chair had been brought with her from her birthplace in Tennessee. She had a corncob pipe until she set her bed on fire one night after falling asleep with it lit. Papaw got rid of the pipe. I spent hours entranced by her voice as she reminisced about her time in Tennessee. She built her own still for brewing moonshine during Prohibition. Stories were told of felling trees to provide wood for cooking and warmth. All were received with breathless anticipation.

I am grateful for my years with Papaw and Nannie. There was peace, tenderness, and love in their home. Money for the nonessentials of life was unavailable. *New* clothes came in bags from Goodwill or The Salvation Army. Nannie was an organized housekeeper and an excellent cook.

Coming home from work, Papaw would bypass the house and head straight to the garden. Eagerly watching the clock for his return home, I clamored out the front door to carry his lunch box inside for him. Small feet would trail behind him as he moved through the garden, inspecting the crops, pulling weeds, and squashing any worm daring to venture onto the well-tilled soil.

There was respect for what God and they had provided. No one came to the table without a shirt on and hat off. Papaw prayed before meals but might take the Lord's name in vain later. No one went to church. Discussions about faith did not take place in the home. An inexpensive replica of the Lord's Supper painting by Leonardo da Vinci hung in the dining room. Today, it hangs in my kitchen, a remembrance of them. We did, on occasion, watch gospel singers on TV, which I found less than entertaining.

Papaw watched the evening news while devouring the newspaper. Read earlier in the day by Nannie, it had been carefully refolded and put on his chair where it respectfully awaited his arrival. Most Saturday evenings, furniture was pushed out of the way, and dancing took place in the family room. Everyone took turns choosing their type of music. Papaw taught me to dance the two-step. A mere wisp of a girl with scraggly blonde hair, my hero took me in his arms to dance. I adored my grandparents. In later years, they came to know Jesus.

Reflection

Thank you, God, for those years with my grandparents. Thank you for the example of love, peace, and tenderness. This comparison of good versus the evil lurking ahead was a gift from You.

And a harvest of righteousness is sown in peace
by those who make peace.
(James 3:18)

Exploring Erikson's Stage Three
The Crisis: Initiative vs. Guilt

[She] must now find out what kind of
person [she] may become.
—E. H. Erikson

Exploration of our environment begins by noticing differences and similarities between people. Language skills and mobility open our horizons to possibilities and increase control of our lives. We evaluate ourselves, ask questions, and develop a view of where we fit into the adult world. We begin to understand when we have done something wrong or right (morality). We require the freedom to imagine what we might become. Opportunities to socialize with other children the same age and older assist with social skills. There is curiosity in noticing differences in people—age, size, race, male, or female. We adjust our social skills as we force ourselves into the domain of the adult world.

A temporary over-curiosity about genital excitement is likely. This typically goes unnoticed by others and seems to pass quickly. Internal feelings of guilt will surface. This sexual awakening often drives a mimicking of a same-sex parental role, typically our mother, via playing with dolls.

Parents should minimize their feelings of failure to measure up to their expectations and extreme guilt for wrongs. Continued growth with a secure parental role is essential. At this stage, it is common for boys to attach to their mothers and girls to attach to their fathers.

As we observe our role models, hypocrisy can cause severe damage. Realizing parents do not follow the rules we have been taught to embrace can lead to the development of "deep regressions and lasting resentments." We "come to feel that the whole matter is not one of universal goodness but arbitrary power . . . Morality can become synonymous with vindictiveness and with the suppression of others."[1] Hypocrisy can lead to distrust and a lack of respect for authority.

Parents should guide us to understand *play* versus reality. Working alongside both parents will assist as the underlying guilt is placed at an appropriate balance for adulthood: "I am what I can imagine I will be."[2]

Reflection

My grandparents served me well during this stage. I received encouragement to explore and imagine possibilities. But the conflicting information about God's role in a person's life was crippling. Failures in stages one and two inhibited my full achievement in stage three.

Triage Questions

1. What are some of your successes and failures during stage three?

2. Where can you see the hand of God during those years—the sweet moments?

3. What failures continue to impact you today?

> Your word is a lamp to my feet
> and a light to my path.
> (Psalm 119:105)

No parent is perfect. Your home might have been stable, but you experienced chaos during extended family events. We are all unique and process our childhood experiences differently. Examining these areas helps us understand the impact of past wounds on how we function today and make life decisions. We seek to understand how these events hold us in bondage, then ask God to break those chains. As God rescues, He creates a new level of discernment for us. He aligns our decision process with His will for our lives.

TRIAGE

Take a few deep, cleansing breaths. This process is not a race. It is a stroll. Take one small step at a time. It's okay to move a mountain of dirt with a teaspoon. God continues to transport the dirt from my life, and He will do the same for you.

Triage Prayer

Father, thank You for calling us daughters. Build within us a desire to move into a closer relationship with You. Release our unmerited guilt, heal the life wounds of years gone by. We know You will carry us on eagle's wings across the barren land stretching before us.

In Jesus's name, Amen

Chapter 4
Why Do I Feel Inferior?

> **Stage Four: Five to Twelve**

Completion of the Formative Years

To this day, I praise God with gratitude for my sweet stage three and a brief moment of sanity at the beginning of my stage four. God knew what lay ahead of me.

As you read stage four, focus on your affirmation versus feelings of inferiority. I'll begin with three of my sweet moments. Remember to include yours in your notes.

Air refused to move on that hot Texas day. Cicadas and katydids sang songs. My sister Marilyn, a neighbor girl, and I (age six) walked the railroad tracks. Arms extended, the tracks became a poor girl's balance beam. Three barefooted girls were on a trek without a care in the world. The tracks took a dip, moving to the shape of the ground as if laid on what was once a creek bed.

We stepped off the tracks, stretched on our tiptoes, and leaned against the dirt-walled embankment. Three little heads strained to see above the top edge of the ditch. What a wonderland of watermelons we discovered. A plan of attack began to unfold. My accomplices pushed my backside to assist in my climb up the embankment. I slithered under the rusty barbed-wired fence and crept forward into the patch.

What a sight for the farmer. My backside popped up as I heaved the melon, attempting to move it forward. It rolled back and forth, refusing to cooperate until the sound of a shotgun in the distance generated adrenaline. Without an option, the watermelon snapped from its vine and ran for its life. It plunged under the fence, down the embankment, with me in hot pursuit. The railroad tracks forced an abrupt halt as it smashed and burst open. Mission accomplished, I sat on the tracks to consume the best melon ever.

The 1960s presented racial discrimination in ways that baffled the mind. Water-fountain signage denoted drinking separation based on race. The school's introduction of integration marked those years. The first girl of color in my elementary school was ostracized. Teachers placed her on the far side of the cafeteria at a table by herself. No one was allowed near her. My heart broke for her heart. Nothing reflected God's love.

For a man of those times, Papaw enjoyed a unique relationship with the Black community beyond the woods. Amid global racial unrest, mutual respect was experienced. I recall the year when late rains brought a bumper crop of green beans, okra, purple-hulled peas, and more. The bounty of the harvest and canning season was behind us. Nooks and crannies were filled with Mason jars. Opening the linen closet, you might find green beans or peaches.

Papaw sat before daybreak, enjoying his Saturday morning coffee. He stood to look out the window, checking to see if the weatherman's prediction was correct. Folks from the Black community lined the road in front of the house. He grabbed an additional cup of coffee and walked out the front door. He glanced at me as if to say, "Have you girls been up to mischief again?" Wide-eyed and innocent, my face answered *no, sir*. I tagged along. If Papaw was on the move, so was I. He handed the extra cup of coffee to their spokesman. "Can you spare any of the bumper crops?" the man asked. Papaw shook his hand and said, "Take all you can find," then turned and walked back to the house.

My eyes searched his to understand the transaction. "These are workin' folk just like us. Not askin' for a handout, askin' if they can work," he explained. Looking over my shoulder, I witnessed their smiling faces as they gathered the crops. This attitude of respecting work ethic, not color, along with the song "Jesus Loves the Little Children," forever shaped my view of racial discrimination. Thank You, God, for opening the eyes and heart of a little girl.

How was I introduced to Jesus? Patent leather shoes became Marilyn's heart's desire. At age nine, she knew how to get them. We were going to church. Older sisters are brilliant. A half mile west sat a missionary Baptist church comprised of about twenty-five older ladies. Uphill to the east rested a Pentecostal church, also small but more entertaining.

Marilyn knew our grandparents would not let us attend church without a special dress and patent leather shoes. Marilyn was a genius. Or maybe not. She was right; Nannie purchased the shoes. We alternated churches each Sunday. But growing feet began to push into those shiny shoes. Pinched toes and blisters resulted. The proximity to the Baptist church became a better plan.

Reflection

Isn't it wonderful how God uses the simplest things, like the desire for patent leather shoes, to draw us to Him? God loved me so much that He called me to Him. He knew the horrors ahead of me and how much I would need Him.

TRIAGE

*He predestined us for adoption to himself
as sons through Jesus Christ,
according to the purpose of his will.
(Ephesians 1:5)*

*Keep me as the apple of your eye; hide me in
the shadow of your wings, from the wicked
who do me violence, my deadly enemies
who surround me.
(Psalm 17:8–9)*

The sweet little church could not afford air-conditioning or Sunday school books. The King James Bible language confused me. It puzzled me when the pastor worked himself into a frenzy and dabbed sweat from his brow. But I loved the songs about Jesus. Music continues to pierce my soul in both sorrowful and joyful ways.

Three years later, on Easter Sunday, I understood Jesus loved me so much that He died for my sins so I could be in His family. This shy, quiet little girl was pulled out of my comfort zone. It felt like a giant magnet pulled me as I ran down the aisle. My baptism took place the next week, ending any guidance from the church on how to live a Christian life until adulthood.

Spiritual discussions did not exist in the home. The oversized family Bible, used to document births, weddings, and deaths, remained forbidden to little hands. Evening prayer became a part of my daily routine. Nannie encouraged us to say, "Now I lay me down to sleep, I pray the Lord my soul to keep. If I should die before I wake, I pray the Lord my soul to take." What did these words mean? I continued to pray out of respect for Nannie. Added to these words were, "Please stop Marilyn. She punches my arm when I annoy her. And, please feed hungry children." The poor, hungry children, spoken about in church, weighed on my heart.

My child's mind could not unravel the evolution of life's next step. Unaware, there had been a decision for me to live with Aunt Pat and Uncle Marvin in Virginia. Uncle Marvin was Mama's older brother. Marilyn would continue to live with Nannie and Papaw. Their realization of Mama's ongoing needs presented concerns. The unknown financial and physical energies required troubled them. No explanations were given to me concerning my new living arrangements. This sent my imagination swirling.

Thoughts came to me: I had complained to Nannie about an uncle, one of Mama's brothers, who sexually fondled me. Were they trying to protect me? Had I caused problems by telling? I knew Papaw had given him a talking-to.

My childish intuition created internal dialogues. Feelings of rejection and guilt took root. I carried the issue on my tiny shoulders.

What other reason could there be for sending me away? These and other ideas pushed into my thoughts. Satan had found his way into the abyss of my insecurities from earlier years. Years of fear, doubt, and lack of trust in myself and others rose to the surface. I began to mentally process the potential reasons for my impending departure from the only home I had known.

I knew they loved me. I tried to be a sweet little girl. Had I failed? Marilyn seemed confused, unable to provide answers. Although I am choosing not to share the details of the molestation by my uncle, I do want to share part of the damage. What seemed a lack of rescue after the fondling planted seeds of my unworthiness of respect. My opinion of how girls obtain love shifted, particularly from men.

The drive from Texas to Virginia was pleasant and uneventful. I missed my life in Texas. But Aunt Pat showed thoughtfulness toward me and eased the transition. They lived in a two-bedroom mobile home. Gone during the day, Uncle Marvin served in the Navy at Norfolk, VA.

While at the store with Aunt Pat, I stole a candy bar. Once home, the theft was soon discovered, and we went back to the store. I sought forgiveness from the manager and accepted his graciousness. Thank you, Aunt Pat. You required me to own my sin. What a great life lesson.

As suddenly as I was sent to Virginia, the plan for my return to Texas presented itself. Overheard conversations suggested strained expenses. Years later, I discovered the truth: They were divorcing. At age nine, I began to view myself as a problem. Why did it cost so much? Just tell me what to do. Please don't send me away. After two short months in Virginia, I traveled to Texas on the Greyhound bus.

The bus trip from Virginia to Texas covered 1,400 miles, involved multiple stops and transfers to other buses, and required three full days of travel. Again rejected, I thought, *Will Papaw and Nannie be ashamed of me for this rejection? What will Mama think? Please, God, do You still love me?*

God's protection is a marvel. Greyhound bus changes took place in dark underground terminals. The giant world of restaurants, terminal navigation, and a forced interface with strangers bred new insecurities. This timid country girl stood fiddling with the hem of her skirt, avoiding eye contact. I *marvel* that only men helped me along the way. Isn't it strange? I recall women on the bus, but only men came to my aid. A sailor held my hand, waiting with me to ensure I transferred to the correct bus.

A bus driver bought me something to eat. Tears welled, and my frightened face said everything: *This place is big and scary. Why is everyone talking so loud? I've never read a menu or decided what I want. Please help me.* He began to read the menu high above the countertop. The first item, a scrambled egg sandwich, received a "yes." Anything to end the torment. We sat facing each other as I ate the driest sandwich ever. I could see his nervousness build while I choked it down. Poor guy kept checking his watch every few minutes. In later years, I often wondered why only men watched over me. I learned later that Hebrews 1:14 tells of how God promises to send us ministering angels.

In Texas, I encountered plan B. My new destination was Mama's youngest sister, Linda. I would live with her, her husband, Marvin, and their nine-month-old boy. Again, no explanations were given. On the drive to Dallas, Linda turned from the front seat, handed me the baby, and said, "This is your job." Startled, I had to remind myself to breathe.

Reflection

God pulled me to Him before this transition so I could walk these years with Him at my side and to keep me from the very depths of mental collapse. Thank you, Marilyn. Your desire for patent leather shoes took us to church, where I met Jesus.

In the discussions about where I should go, the uncle who sexually fondled me and his wife contemplated taking me. Thank You, God, for sending me to the lesser of the two evils.

> *Give ear to my words, O LORD; consider my groaning.*
> *Give attention to the sound of my cry,*
> *my King and my God, for to you do I pray.*
> *(Psalm 5:1–2)*

> *Look among the nations, and see; wonder*
> *and be astounded. For I am doing a work in your*
> *days that you would not believe if told.*
> *(Habakkuk 1:5)*

I struggle to explain those next seven years. It started with a silence that permeated the entire three-hour car ride to Dallas. Lack of air-conditioning required windows to be down. Highway sounds filtered in to break a fraction of the tension. The baby seemed comfortable and happy to rest on my lap. But no warmth or extended words of kindness came from the front seat to the back. The atmosphere was frightening. It was late evening when we arrived at my new home, a two-story fourplex on a crowded inner-city Dallas street. My eyes searched for my bed. The sheets hit me on my back so hard that I lost my balance. "I knew you were stupid! Put those on the couch" came from Linda. And so it began.

Unfamiliar noises filtered through the apartment walls. Neighbors went about their daily lives, cars created street noises, people in their yards smiled and called to one another a hello, and the occasional raised voices of neighbors could be heard. These new and strange occurrences did not scare me, but my daily life with twenty-one-year-old Linda terrified me.

The next morning, Marvin went to work. I would be hard-pressed to find anyone who didn't like Marvin. His gentle nature and constant smile drew folks in. However, he brought a new emphasis to the term *people-pleasing*. I would later discover his awareness of Linda's actions. He refused to intervene for fear of the conflict.

On the other hand, Linda defined cruelty. We can start with the Cinderella aspects of a nine-year-old required to get up at 4:00 a.m. I bathed and fed the baby, washed the dishes, and swept floors. The laundry I started the night before needed to be hung on the clotheslines before going to school.

For the first time in my life, I wet the bed. Linda tied my soiled pajamas around my neck and invited unwary neighbors for snacks and tea. She paraded me around, wearing the soiled pajamas, and introduced me as the bed wetter. My broken heart physically ached. An invisible knife plunged inside my chest. Demoralized and humiliated, I mentally withdrew into myself. The building of emotional protective walls began. These mental walls were needed if I was to survive her insanity and abuse.

She complained about the bed-wetting to Nannie as if damaged goods had been pawned off on her. This generated a visit to the doctor. While I lay with my legs spread open, Linda stood in the corner of the exam room. She smirked with sheer delight at my continued humiliation. He found nothing physically wrong to cause the issue. The bed-wetting stopped within months.

Through the years, a love for hanging out the clothes grew, except for winter months. There was no outside playtime, and I was an outdoor-loving girl. Hanging the laundry out shielded me from her, providing a temporary escape from her wrath, a fury manifested in varied ways. The winter months found me standing on my toes, stretching to reach the lines, blood draining toward my shoulders. Bright red fingers prickled from the cold, wet clothes. The numbness of my hands made it more difficult to open the clothespins. The clothes waited for my removal until I returned from school. Frozen or damp clothes started the laundry process again, with washing and hanging out.

Diapers were labor-intensive. My child's lack of hand strength pushed this process into hours. The residual feces were rinsed into the toilet; diapers were soaked in the bathtub and wrung. This was followed by draining and refilling the tub and soaking them again.

Wrung again, they were put into the washer and finally ready to hang outside. If they did not pass inspection, violence ensued.

I sobbed myself to sleep for years, begging, begging God to rescue me. I dreamed of Daddy as a kind, godly man, sweeping me into his arms and stealing me away. He did not. Hanging out clothes became my world of fantasies. I daydreamed Marilyn would turn eighteen, storm through the door, and rescue me. I often fantasized God would change Linda. God did not.

Linda manipulated Papaw and Nannie to get money, requiring frequent trips to visit. Money given toward perceived needs disappeared to accommodate Linda's wants. Marvin took a second job.

Linda could not leave me behind on these visits. What would Papaw, Nannie, and Mama think? So, she made terrifying threats if I shared my life. But I told Marilyn, and she listened as I recounted Linda's anger. I shared that she told me she did not want me; she wanted Marilyn. She listened as I listed housework demands, childcare, no time for homework, and the face-slaps or yanking me across the room by my hair. Punishments for not cleaning something, the lack of sleep, and more. It brought comfort to know Marilyn believed me. She knew the tenderness of my heart.

Marilyn shared our conversations with Nannie. No help was given. The extended family knew of issues in the home. They didn't know everything, but they knew it was bad. No one rode in on a white horse to rescue me. It is an unfortunate reality for families. With good hearts, folks remain unwilling to step into conflict. They know this type of conflict often divides the family. The foreseen risk of family strife is too high.

TRIAGE

Reflection

Thank You, Father, for the comfort Marilyn provided. Thank You. The bed-wetting stopped.

> *For I will satisfy the weary soul, and every*
> *languishing soul I will replenish.*
> *(Jeremiah 31:25)*

> *Two are better than one, because they have*
> *a good reward for their toil. For if they fall,*
> *one will lift up his fellow. But woe to him*
> *who is alone when he falls and*
> *has not another to lift him up!*
> *(Ecclesiastes 4:9–10)*

Linda's cruelty persisted, and the years went by. Grocery shopping became my added responsibility. My frail arms struggled to carry the heavy-laden paper bags. They often tore, giving way for groceries to roll down the sidewalk.

The vicious mental games continued, along with slaps, yanked hair, kicks, and verbal abuse. And the control, control, control of my every move. She hated me. Her expression lacked any tenderness. Venomously, she scowled at me through angry eyes, furrowed brow, and downturned mouth. How could so much evil exist in a person?

She screened my regular letters to Mama to ensure I communicated my wonderful home life. Rare opportunities popped up, allowing me to slip a note for Marilyn inside the envelope. Marilyn signified a fragile lifeline to love and hope. I hoped I could make it until I turned eighteen.

In May 1966, Marilyn's graduation from eighth grade spurred a visit. At Papaw and Nannie's home, Linda played the role of mother to her sons. Although I loved the children, those respites furnished my childhood with the ability to breathe. I slipped away to spend time with Marilyn and Mama. I did not speak with Mama about my home life. I felt sorry for her and believed it would only bring additional grief.

Excitement permeated the day and evening. Preparation for Marilyn's graduation had the whole house buzzing. They piled her long brown hair high on her head. She morphed from a girl to a sophisticated, glamorous woman. A simple knee-length white dress was selected for the occasion. I saw her as stunning. She was my big sister, and I adored her. She pulled me aside and for the first time in my life said, "I love you." It warmed my heart down to my soul. I knew she felt bad for me.

The ceremony finished, and the family loaded into cars. Marilyn, beaming with joy, ran to Nannie's car window. She asked permission to attend a celebration bonfire party at the lake. Mama and I sat silently in the back seat. Marilyn's young man of interest would drive them there and bring her home. She and her young man headed off with the other graduates, elated by the permission granted. He was seventeen, and it was a week before her fifteenth birthday.

Hours went by without her return. Notification to the police made things more real. Officially a missing person, I don't know how to describe the torment of those days. Each of us hoped for the best but thought the worst. Abduction? Abused?

After three sleepless days and nights, fishermen found her body in the lake. The car had gone off the road, plunging into the dark waters. She and her young man both died. Her voice, her smile, wiped from existence. My lifeline to love and sanity evaporated. Devastated by the loss and, once again, feeling abandoned and unworthy of love, I became angry with God. My life history created an angry young woman distrustful of authority, including God. At the age of twelve, I ceased to pray.

Reflection

The loss of my sisters created a massive hole in my heart. It is the reason I have a passion for my sisters in Christ. God always has a plan.

Exploring Erikson's Stage Four Crisis: Industry vs. Inferiority

During this stage, we learn to manage wins and losses. Lack of positive support can lead to feelings of inferiority. We begin developing the need for productivity (industry), social skills become a priority, and we fantasize about future jobs and role-play.

We now better understand what tools are required to perform desired tasks. From crayons and scissors to hair ribbons and ways to curl our hair, we can decide what we need. We discover the power of a smile, a compliment, and the weight of expressing our disdain. We have grown in our realization of what is needed. Cause and effect are comprehended; we achieve better grades if we study. Encouragement by parents and teachers is critical. Observing people in authority going about their jobs, skilled workers, and office workers gives insight into our possibilities.

We become aware of the connection between recognition received and the accomplishment of a task. Failures from stage three will lead to feelings of inferiority and a *desire to return to stage three* to gain needed skills. We will discover likes/dislikes and evaluate our expertise compared to peers and siblings. These comparisons to peers in the school environment bring an awareness of skills we attained or those left unattained. If unprepared, the demands of stage four may heighten guilt. We notice the initiative lost during our stage three.

Concerning education, "Where [she] finds out immediately, however, that the color of [her] skin or the background of [her] parents rather than [her] wish and will to learn, are the factors that decide [her] worth as a pupil or apprentice, the human propensity for feeling unworthy may be fatefully aggravated as a determinant of character development."[1] Race, poverty, and culture can impact how we see ourselves and what we believe we can achieve.

Our influencers must balance when to press for excellence, when to encourage, and when to pause while they provide instruction. These years should allow us to discover at least one thing we do well. Were we allowed to connect the world of play to the "product of reality, practicality, and logic"?[2]

At risk is a rigid learning environment, where too much emphasis on task/reward is overly conforming. You may become an easily exploitable conformist. This held for me. I conformed to the dictators in my life.

Triage Questions

1. My stage four bred inferiority and a longing to retreat to my stage three. How would you describe your stage four? Were you industrious (did you believe you could be productive)? Were you confident in exploring your possibilities?

2. Did this stage contribute to your desire to please others? If so, how does it manifest today?

Reflection

I grew up confused about God and religion. The church preached a legalistic standard of living. If I played cards, danced, wore slacks, cut my hair, wore makeup, or pierced my ears, I was going to hell, burning for eternity. I felt constant judgment from the church.

During my years with Nannie and Papaw, we only prayed before meals. We danced and played games. They drank on occasion, and no discussions about God took place.

I have since learned the love and power of a relationship with Jesus. Life with Linda was living with evil. Years later, I realized how God protected my heart and mind during those years. We have a great, great God. He restores our brokenness. Lean on Him.

Triage Prayer

Father, we acknowledge, with gratitude, Your goodness. You perfectly created each of us. You do not make mistakes. Remove any residual feelings of unworthiness, inferiority, and the desire to please a world we will never please. Direct us to clarity and courage as we revisit our wounds. Heal us, Jehovah Rapha, God of all healing. May everything we do bring glory to You.

The waters closed in over me to take my life; the deep surrounded me;
weeds were wrapped about my head at the roots of the mountains.
I went down to the land whose bars closed upon me forever,
yet you brought up my life from the pit, O Lord my God.
When my life was fainting away, I remembered the Lord,
and my prayer came to you, into your holy temple.
(Jonah 2:5-7)

In Jesus's name, Amen

Chapter 5
Who Am I? Finding My Identity

Stage Five: Twelve to Eighteen

Beyond the Formative Years

When we turn from God, we surrender the possibility of joy. I ceased to pray at the end of stage four, so the presence of God was not felt. His power and mercy remained shielded from my mind and soul, but He carried my burdens and preserved my sanity for His future plans. Sometimes, we can't see the sweet moments amid struggles. My sweet moments escaped recognition, and my youth slipped away.

Linda's influence inserted the power for stage five to dismantle the remnants of my heart. At the time, I didn't feel God's help, but without His protection, I surely would have lost my mind or worse. Although I told God, "I hate you," He still loved me. Writing these words of hate toward God brings tears.

Revealing the primary causes of your early years' issues will help you understand the hurts God needs to address. What burdens do you carry? Begin to transfer those to Him through prayer. He did not create you to shoulder the weight of this world. Are you spending this season in prayer for yourself? Reading your Bible?

Your evaluation of the harms and their impact is viewed through the lens of intentionality. The damage assessment does not, by default, indicate it was intentional. Nannie and Papaw did not intend to cause me harm. Linda set out to destroy me.

The crisis in this stage pertains to your identity. For example, are you comfortable with how others see you? Is your approval dependent on how others view you? Do you allow people to serve as your judge? My inability to fit in with those around me took its toll until I realized that the only opinion that matters is God's. Does He look at me and say, "Well done, my daughter"?

As I present my stage five, watch the impact of trust issues, insecurities, feelings of rejection, and others on my failure to succeed in this stage. Think about your previous stages. Did they adequately prepare you for this stage? Did your stage five help or hinder how you currently formulate your decisions?

Marilyn's funeral was behind me, and life with Marvin and Linda returned to normal. Marvin, employed by an investor, opened restaurants around the US. We moved often for the next year. Frequent moves did not represent a change. Linda, dissatisfied with her station in life, insisted we try a different apartment every year.

My social skills suffered additional damage due to my attendance at ten schools by age sixteen. Labeled the "new kid" in school, I learned to survive alone, friendless. My safeguard against the world, secrecy became my friend. I bore a shroud of unearned shame.

Marvin's last relocation returned us to Dallas. We moved several more times before buying a small three-bedroom, one-bath house. Most teens would be excited to transition from apartment to house, but it signaled more square footage for me to clean. Once a month, I mowed the weeds of the sad little yard. Manicured lawns around it brought attention to its condition. I recoiled in embarrassment.

My body began to show adult development. Linda saw a boy take notice of me and called me a whore. The word required a search in the dictionary. This first branding stung. It was a new form of a slap. She remained alert for the next opportunity to demean and wound my heart. Future labels held little power. I kept a dictionary handy to interpret the latest vile thing she called me.

Marvin worked a full-time job and two part-time jobs. I struggled to understand where all the money went. At age thirteen, Linda insisted I get a full-time job cooking at the restaurant with Marvin. She forged my signature on paychecks, often going places to meet men. She had an affair the prior year, which sent Marvin into a temporary tailspin. But they worked it out. She wanted money; I represented the means.

With the job, I had hoped for a reduction in household responsibilities. Relief did not come. I continued to get up at 4:00 a.m. to take care of the Cinderella things. I attended school two days per week. On days not in school, I took care of the household demands. When at school, I slept through most of my classes. I worked over sixty hours per week at the restaurant. Exhausted and friendless, I attended no school activities.

Isolation was my best friend. It helped me build stronger walls of protection and a mental numbness. These fortifications brought comfort and safety from a world sure to recognize my unworthiness to join them. My imagined contemptibility solidified my surrender for the struggle to acknowledge my wants and needs. Learning to minimize my life desires cushioned the impact of daily mental blows to my psyche. It was easier to agree; I held no worth. My mind could not process the reality of my life. Anger toward God continued. Later, my committed walk with Jesus allowed Him to restore my view of my worth.

Reflection

Thank You, Father, You never forget those who belong to You.

For I know the plans I have for you, declares the LORD, plans for welfare and not for evil, to give you a future and a hope. Then you will call upon me and come and pray to me, and I will hear you. You will seek me and find me, when you seek me with all your heart. I will be found by you, declares the LORD, and I will restore your fortunes and gather you from all the nations and all the places where I have driven you, declares the LORD, and I will bring you back to the place from which I sent you into exile.
(Jeremiah 29:11–14)

At sixteen, I met an eighteen-year-old young man. We worked at the same restaurant alongside Marvin. He flattered me, and I functioned as a sponge, soaking it in. With Marvin and Linda's permission, we began dating. A month later, Marvin and Linda went out for dinner. I stood in the kitchen busy with cleanup after the kiddos were fed, bathed, and tucked into bed.

Then, the oddest thing happened. They came through the front door. My back to them, hands in the sink, I heard Linda say my boyfriend's name. I turned with a smile from ear to ear. She said, "See! She's in love. We need to plan a wedding now!" Marriage? This had not occurred to me, but I jumped on board. My refusal to engage in premarital sex led to his proposal. Let's not give me too much credit for the morality of not engaging in sexual activity. I did not want to risk a pregnancy and give Linda access to my child.

The impending nuptials dictated a trip. He needed to meet Papaw, Nannie, and Mama. Although not thrilled with the young man, Papaw did not say no. Giddy best describes my emotional state. He provided attention, and I felt significant. We would live happily ever after and have lots of kiddos for me to love. I lived in a dream. Good grief.

Linda planned and executed the wedding within a month. My attempt to discuss completion of high school met with an adamant no. Linda led the discussion, but Marvin said nothing to overrule her. One month after the start of the eleventh grade, I dropped out.

A week after the wedding, I returned to collect my belongings. Before we married, I had moved a few clothes into our first home, a tiny one-bedroom furnished apartment. During the week, Linda held a yard sale planned well in advance. My things had disappeared except my sewing machine, a gift from Papaw and Nannie. Disposal of it would generate disapproval from them. I gathered it and left.

I soon became better acquainted with my rescuer, my husband. He created a new definition of control and abuse. The bruises on his mother's face gave testimony of his father's battery. Daily outbursts took the form of screams inches from my face. The threat of this level of physical abuse got my attention. Most days, I took two birth control pills to ensure I would not get pregnant. Yes, two. The brilliance of being sixteen.

I came home from work one evening to find him and a friend on the sofa. The number of scattered empty beer cans gave evidence of trouble on the way. The taunts began with, "Show us what ya got? Come on, baby, just a little dance. You can do better than that." Tension built, tones became harsh, "Don't embarrass me! I said dance." The escalation transitioned into threats of violence. Tears streaming, I made it through one song on the radio before I fled into the bedroom and locked the door. My labored breaths forced through gut-wrenching sobs. Humiliated, frightened, and violated, this threat was a different intensity. I feared for my life.

Next came the push for a threesome. Refusals to bring another woman into our bed generated explosions of anger riddled with threats of physical ramifications. One night, frightened, I pretended to agree. Watching his every movement, I inched my way to the door. Grabbing my purse and keys, I fled. Blinded by tears, I sped through the streets with no destination. Failure to notice the first lights behind me led to multiple police cars circling to block my path. Incoherent blurts of information gave them the basics of my situation. They escorted me back home and gave him a stern lecture. Not helpful. It was all they could do under the circumstances. God's gift to me was the lack of my arrest for speeding and the failure to stop.

It didn't take long for me to become our sole support. He would work for short periods, weeks, or a few months, then quit. His earnings were spent on a race car and other silliness to amuse himself. Paychecks disappeared for bowling or billiards. Continued frustration by my refusal to bring other women into our bed brought daily unleashed anger. Jealous scenes were created at my job. "Who were you talking to? I bet you'll be with him on your break." The other things said are not appropriate for this book. These outbursts regularly led to my loss of employment and a move on to the next job.

Three years into the marriage, he abandoned me, taking what money we had and our only operable car. He had neglected to pay rent for several months. I came home to find the apartment door had been bolted for nonpayment, with my belongings inside. It was a beautiful, warm November day when I left that morning. I wore jeans, a lightweight chambray shirt, and sneakers with no socks as I walked the streets searching for a job. Without a battery in my car and a gradual loss of air in the tires, I searched on foot. The instant he abandoned me, the car became my shelter. I was homeless.

The following day, winter reared its head. Days and months passed as the temperatures dropped. My daily walks took me to fast-food restaurants and grocery stores in search of a job. The early 1970s experienced inflation, recession, and high unemployment. My lack of a high school diploma did not help.

I washed in a nearby gas station restroom. Restrooms did not require a key to gain access back then, and soap dispensers did not exist. The soap came in the form of an abrasive bar and sucked any remnant of moisture from my skin. Before using the bar, the last person's grime had to be scrubbed off. I found it easier to wash the top half of my body one day and the lower half the next. Washing hair was complicated. The filthy sink needed to be cleaned first. Yes, yuck. Yet another challenge was the number of paper towels required for this bathing process. Towels scattered on the floor protected my bare feet from the disgusting linoleum.

When I washed my bottom half, I washed my panties, dried them in paper towels, then put them back on still damp. With winter temperatures, bathing half of my body helped minimize my risk of hypothermia. Brushing teeth was accomplished with my index finger and water.

Then, and now, I find glimpses of the positives in my life. My contentment develops around God's *chosen* provision, not what I think I need. My mental health, what there was of it, was protected in part by pressing into gratitude. My life reflects a desire to find gratitude in the middle of strife. Satisfaction frees me from comparisons to others' lives. Here's the good and the bad of my car life. Good, the car sat in the apartment parking lot, a low-crime area. Good, my husband would not show up as we owed the apartment complex money. Good, it blocked the wind and kept me dry on rainy nights. Bad, there was no blanket, coat, or anything to provide warmth. I burrowed into the backseat and curled into a fetal position in an attempt to capture my body heat.

Before the abandonment, I sporadically attended a local church. Once I became homeless, I spoke with the pastor and asked for assistance with a car battery. I wanted to expand my pursuit of a job. He stared at me sternly and replied, "We do not approve of women in the workplace." He provided no help. My impression of

Christians and the church remained damaged for years by this single occurrence.

On one of my daily searches for a job, I noticed the construction of new apartments. I knew I would not be suitable for the front office; I was a mess. As I opened the door to the office, I saw a young woman at the desk. She was my age, smiling and laughing with other people in the office, not a care in the world. The clothes fit well, and her hair and makeup were perfectly done. She eyed me from head to toe as if she had eaten something distasteful. Thankfully, she hired me as a housekeeper. Grateful for the work, I did not have bad thoughts about her. At eighteen, I'm not sure I would have responded differently to the sight of me.

My job as a housekeeper directed me to clean the apartments under construction. On rare occasions, I cleaned an occupied apartment. As workers completed a section of apartments, I readied them for leasing. Oh my, those apartments were the filthiest you can imagine. Workmen's greasy tools were tossed into tubs for cleaning. Urine and feces might be found anywhere.

I scraped the over-sprayed paint off the outside windows with a razor blade. I had no coat, gloves, or socks. The freezing, windy cold of late December and January bit my body. My fingers transitioned from pinpricks to numb. My five-foot-three, ninety-five-pound body hauled cleaning supplies and an upright vacuum up and down two and three flights of stairs, up and down, up and down. I continued to sleep in my car. Over the winter, all four tires went flat. Still, there was no battery. Thankfully, the apartment manager did not tow my car. Thank You, Jesus. This job allowed for one meat and bean burrito daily. I saved for a battery and what I thought would be tire repair.

The question I often get asked is, "Why did you not contact family?" The only people I considered family were over two hundred miles away, my grandparents. Their responsibilities for Mama were demanding. How could I add to their burdens? I see it differently now. But at the time, I was so ashamed. How could a decent woman end up married to someone so horrible? Without God, we think nonsensical things. And, in those days, there was a stigma around divorce. Society viewed women who divorced as women of loose values. I had gotten myself into the mess. I needed to get myself out.

Reflection

Our Lord saw me and did not allow anyone to harm me as I lived homeless. Thank You, oh great Protector.

> *But I will sing of your strength; I will sing aloud*
> *of your steadfast love in the morning.*
> *For you have been to me a fortress and a*
> *refuge in the day of my distress.*
> *(Psalms 59:16)*

Thank You for the power found in Your love and wisdom. I am not responsible for others' behavior, only mine.

The following spring, my spouse contacted his parents. They asked, "Where's your wife?" He was forced to explain that he had left me months earlier. His dad went to the apartment and saw my broken-down car. When I showed up, he took me to buy a battery and put air in the tires. My job options were broadened. I moved in with them for a month while desperately searching for work. My soon-to-be ex was not around.

Exploring Erikson's Stage Five Crisis: Identity vs. Role Confusion

Physical changes drive us into puberty; our body demands entrance into adulthood. Mental and emotional growth strive to keep up. Peers have more influence than adult role models. Hormones, body changes, dating, crushes, and decisions on future careers all place demands on us as a teen. An inability to settle on potential future occupational goals will present disturbances for us. Often, our identities are forfeited as we trade them for peers or *heroes*. Cliques become destructive to the participants as well as the rejected.

"Ideologically" minded, she meshes "the morality learned [as a] child, and the ethics to be developed by the adult."[1]

These ideological minds are susceptible to manipulation by governments and predators. Allowing us to experiment with hair, clothes, and makeup helps us discover who we will become. Forced adult values can lead to rebellion when we leave home if not gently managed during these years.

Teens need boundaries, but they also need freedom to explore. This stage resembles infancy as we once again take those first shaky steps. We need encouragement, guidance, and love. Unconditional love.

Reflection

Thank You, Father. You used my teen husband's hard heart as You used Pharaoh's. He is now on the National Sex Registry as a pedophile. Thank You, thank You for those birth control pills. Homelessness was a small price to be free of him.

*They are darkened in their understanding, alienated
from the life of God because of the ignorance
that is in them, due to their hardness of heart.
(Ephesians 4:18)*

Triage Questions

1. Puberty is a time of uncertainty. Think of your teen years and the possibilities of who you could have become. In what ways did peers help you with the uncertainties surrounding your life's possibilities?

2. In what ways did your peers disappoint you?

3. Whether positive or negative, how did this stage help define your view of your identity?

4. On a 1 to 5 scale, where 5 is very confident, what was your confidence level as you approached adulthood?

5. What has helped you to overcome your stage five issues?

6. We need a willingness to compromise. It is not good to believe we should always get our way. However, when this stage is incomplete, a conflict between compromise and forfeiting what we know is right can emerge. What you deem correct versus others' opinions may be at odds. You may feel bullied. Perhaps your past decisions were driven by teen peer pressure. What directs your decision process now? Peers, past experiences, God, or something else?

Triage Prayer

Father, mend our broken hearts, minds, and souls. Show us our identity is in You and the power of the cross where You bore our sins. Shed our insecurities that were formed when we were teens. Grant us courage and wisdom to make sound life decisions. Surround us with sisters in Christ who will love us well. Let them counsel us based on your Word, not the world's opinions. We are daughters of the King. We choose to value ourselves. We ask You to rehabilitate the wounds of our lives.

In Jesus's name, Amen

Section II

Adulthood

Chapter 6
What Drives the Desire to Isolate?

Stage Six: Eighteen to Twenty

Young Adulthood

The young adulthood stage ranges from ages eighteen to thirty-five. Since so much happens during these years, I've broken this stage into four chapters. This chapter examines ages eighteen to twenty.

The exit from stage five with a secure sense of identity of who you are is critical before entering stage six. Stage five should have provided a comfort for how you insert yourself into society. I should have a sense of "I have control" over decisions that impact my life. I am fascinated by how this aligns with God's design for us. He created us with free will; some choices will be right, others wrong. But He wants us to decide for ourselves. Stage six has additional variables that we will dissect later, but let's focus on two concepts now: your ability to love and whether you prefer to isolate yourself.

I am a person who tends to withdraw, but God's love pulls me out of seclusion and into the world.

Have you seized upon the after-effects of your traumas and how they impact your decision-making process? Do you see the influence of broken stages? We often function well in many areas while we struggle with relationships. For example, I persevered and found employment. I could manage financial resources for necessities. I was responsible, had a good work ethic, and paid the bills. But my relationship choices were a nightmare. Let's continue.

January 1974 was the scheduled opening date for the Dallas-Fort Worth (DFW) airport. The impending opening of DFW created demand in the job market in the spring of 1973. Employee hiring took place early to accommodate training needed for 1974 jobs. I managed to find work with a security company contracted by Braniff Airlines. At the time, Braniff was the top competitor of American Airlines. I turned nineteen in April 1973. Interesting job. Let's think for a moment. What skill set did I possess that qualified me to work as a gun-carrying airport security guard? None.

We worked in pairs, stationed against the wall beside baggage screening. The 1970s experienced over 300 plane hijackings, which spurred the addition of armed guards. The plan was if anyone came through waving weapons, we would shoot them. I know, craziness. A Vietnam veteran partnered with me; at least he knew what to do. They sent us for target practice once. I missed the entire target. Guns owned by the company were checked out at the beginning of our sixteen-hour shift and returned at the end, meaning we received no additional opportunity to practice.

The company provided uniforms with the cost deducted from my first paycheck. The small furnished apartment I rented had no sheets for the bare mattress. The kitchen was void of cooking essentials, and there were no towels. Paper towels came to the rescue. But at least I was warm in my new home. My next check enabled the purchase of sheets, an alarm clock, work shoes, underwear, and socks.

New tires were next on the shopping list. Looking back, I purchased stolen tires. A guy at the apartment complex who worked for a tire company advised me to come by the shop at lunchtime and park at the back of the store. I paid him in cash, and he mounted the tires in ten minutes. Yep, stolen tires.

The inner-city Dallas neighborhood was less than desirable. In later years, it would be reimagined and improved by city leaders. But when I lived in the area, drug dealers, pimps, prostitutes, illegals from all over the world, and drug addicts surrounded me. Despite my neighborhood, I had a strange peace. No one yelled at me, threatened me, or ordered me around.

While in the apartment laundry room, I met Nancy. We quickly became friends. When we were not at work, we sat on the stoop of her apartment, drinking Boone's Farm Strawberry Hill wine and smoking marijuana. I smile at the silliness of my youth. By summer's end, my eyes opened to the truth. Unfettered substance abuse destroyed my neighbors. I did not want to spend my life continuing to spiral downward.

Nancy gave me a small saucepan, a knife, a fork, and a spoon for my barren kitchen. I continued to use them on occasion for another thirty-plus years. They would bring a smile to my heart. Thank you, Nancy, for your kindness. We lost track of each other over time.

Reflection

The Holy Spirit provided the wisdom to see the damage of substance abuse—how kind.

The security company lost its contract with Braniff after a year. A local convenience store in inner-city Dallas became my next job. When you file for divorce in the state of Texas, you are required to provide your current address. This means the other person knows where you live. If you're trying to avoid someone, this doesn't help. My top priority was to make it difficult for him to find me. Renting different apartments every month allowed for frequent moves. It seemed a clever idea.

Fears became a reality when he showed up at my apartment. Banging on the door, he screamed my name. I stood silent on the other side. He gave up but took my car as he left. His brother had come with him, bringing the spare key. The car was in his name. I made the bank payments and all the repairs, but it was his.

I shook away my anger toward him as fast as it arrived. Walking to work was a small price to pay for peace, though I lacked the common sense to recognize the dangers around me and the possibilities of what might happen walking those streets.

For the first time, at nineteen, I controlled my decisions. Previous dictation for my life by one person or another drew to a close. The choices I was about to make did not yield good results, and my inability to discern created a series of horrible decisions that forever changed my life. Wisdom is not an achievement; it is a gift from God.

Exploring Erikson's Stage Six Crisis: Intimacy vs. Isolation

A few things to ponder: Can you sustain friendships and other relationships? Does fear grip you at the thought of emotional bonding? Do you have the discernment to evaluate thriving relationships from destructive ones? Is the power of inspirational teachers (parents, school, church) bonded in your decision process? Establishing your identity in stage five was critical to how you progressed through stage six.

There will still be the heartaches of life as you learn and adjust to sustaining relationships. A secure identity minimizes *catastrophic* relational decisions. The ideological views of life presented in the teen years should have passed. Prince Charming does not exist. A sense of ethics begins to drive these decisions. If you fail to develop wholesome relationships, you may decide to isolate yourself.

"The strength acquired at any stage is tested by the necessity to transcend it in such a way that [you] can take chances in the next stage with what was most vulnerably precious in the previous one."[1]

You need the capacity and ethical strength for committed relationships, both personal and professional. Fear and lack of trust will cause you to pull away from these much-needed adult experiences into isolation.

"The youth who is not sure of [her] identity shies away from interpersonal intimacy or throws [herself] into acts of intimacy which are *promiscuous* without true fusion or real self-abandon."[2] When true relationships are not formed, "[She] may settle for highly stereotyped interpersonal relationships and come to ... isolation."[3]

Although I continue to struggle against isolation, I have learned the value of appropriate friendships. These women know me. They know the good and the ugly yet still love me. They encourage me, cry with me, pray with me, and, in love, tell me when I'm wrong. They do not gossip or speak negatively about their spouses or others. They are not perfect women but are women who are walking toward God, not away from Him.

Reflection

Thank You, Father. You protected this naive young woman as she walked the inner-city streets back and forth to work.

The Lord is my rock and my fortress and my deliverer,
my God, my rock, in whom I take refuge,
my shield, and the horn of my salvation,
my stronghold and my refuge, my savior;
you save me from violence.
(2 Samuel 22:2–3)

Triage Questions

1. Do you have close friendships? If not, what event(s) hinders the development of close relationships?

2. Do you believe God desires us to form relationships with other Christians? If not, why?

3. Have you prayed for God's healing of past and current events? If not, what keeps you from asking for God's help? Write a few words of prayer below. He loves you dearly.

4. Do you struggle with isolation? We should be comfortable with ourselves. Time alone is healthy. However, a preference for isolation is not productive to your well-being. Blessings are discovered when we help others and allow others to assist us. Relationships bring laughter, tears, celebrations, and grief. They bring life. If you withdraw from the world, you miss the growth afforded by lows and the zeal of the highs. What soul damage drives this appeal to isolate?

Triage Prayer

Father, thank You for my sisters in Christ. You created us to be relational. We want to step forward into Your plan and out of our places of fear. Help us to be better friends to others, to love them well. Send us women of God. We need our sisters in Christ.

In Jesus's name, Amen

Chapter 7
Selling Ourselves

Stage Six: Twenty to Twenty-One

Young Adulthood

After the divorce was finalized, I decided to attempt dating. Dating difficulties presented in uncomfortable, awkward shyness, lack of confidence and worth. My mental and emotional downslide plummeted with my first date, a date rape. He took me to dinner and afterward walked me to my door. His thoughtfulness impressed me. Feelings of warmth and security surrounded me. Opening the apartment door, he pushed me inside, into the bedroom, and raped me. Afterward, standing at the door, he turned to ask why I cried through the entire incident. The door closed, and I rushed to lock it. My legs gave way beneath me as I crumbled to the floor in tears.

I crawled back into my shell, and the construction of taller, deeper emotional walls grew. These walls became massive. Built of fear, resentment, anger, and lack of trust, it would take years to knock them down, brick by brick. Today, when they try to rebuild themselves, I press into God's arms; only He can drive them back down.

My convenience store job brought men and their flirtations. I smiled back but shunned their advances. Then he came in. Let's call him "M" for master manipulator. M remarked on the beauty of my hands, paid for his items, and left. These harmless remarks continued over the next few months. When he finally asked me out, we were old friends. He was thoughtful and held back sexual advances. We dated regularly. His job was as assistant manager at a local drug store, and he attended college. The concept of grooming women to gain control was unknown to me. It didn't take a genius to assess my dependence on authority, lack of worth, and zero world experience. A predator's perfect target is someone who identifies as a victim.

There is no rationalization for my next steps. I try to look back and see the battered and bullied young woman, five-foot-three and one hundred pounds if you threw enough water on me. I was content working double shifts with only enough money for essentials. If you have survived with nothing, your mind shifts when you evaluate needs versus wants.

Clarity is best found in the light of day. The evening brings a more relaxed setting. Weary from the day's work, my guard was down, creating a better opportunity for manipulation. Layer on a lack of fellowship with God and my mental woundedness, and the inevitable catastrophe awaited. Satan prowled for his next meal.

M arranged his plan in a smooth, even-toned voice. He carefully placed each word as a flower in a vase. Everything in me screamed, NO! But robotically, my well-oiled mind stepped back under the control of evil. I subjected myself to manipulation and bullying by this new tormentor. "You'll be working in the upscale hotels, not the streets. Businessmen will treat you well, it'll be great. Why not receive payment for what will happen anyway?" From age twenty to twenty-one, I prostituted my dignity, pride, and life away in the best of Dallas's hotels. Satan had me by the throat, and M was his instrument.

One evening, M told me to drive us to the concert. There was no cause for alarm; concerts were a common occurrence. We needed to make two stops, the first at the pharmacy where he worked. "One last errand, then we'll be on our way," he said nonchalantly. We parked in the alley behind the business where his friend worked. Everything went sideways. I was in the middle of a drug sale gone bad.

The summer heat had mandated the windows be open. I was in the driver's seat, and M was in the passenger seat. The friend, now standing at the driver's side door, did not want to pay for the drugs taken from the pharmacy. Suddenly, the buyer's upper body pushed through my window. He waved his gun and demanded the drugs be handed over. My mind drifted to my mother. *Authorities will inform her that her daughter died during a drug deal.* Snapping back to reality, adrenaline forced my mind to operate.

His body pinned me between the seat and the steering wheel. In one smooth motion, I forced my right arm under his body, restarted the engine, threw it into reverse, and slammed the gas pedal, throwing the car backward. He fell out of the window, unable or unwilling to shoot us. The rearview mirror showed him stumbling to his feet. A mile down the road, the adrenaline rush transitioned to sobs and shaking as I pulled the car to the side of the road. M drove us to the concert as if it were a typical day.

A normal person would have ended everything; I didn't see options. How do you function as an adult when your lifetime reflects enslavement? Full of shame, I surrendered to the idea that my life held no value. A year later, at twenty-one, while at a hotel, I cut my left wrist and took a bottle of Valium. Two days later, I awoke. My only thought—*I can't even get that right.*

Back at the apartment we shared, M beat me for my two-day disappearance. For the first time, his violence came at me. The back of his right hand came hard across the right side of my face. His open right hand came across the left side of my face. Berating me worthless, he continued to throw blows. Shocked and terrified, the intuitive withdrawal into a fetal position braced me for the inevitable pull of the trigger. He had retrieved his .38 pistol and aimed it at my head. Pulling the trigger, the gun clicked as if unloaded. He cursed, threw the gun across the room, and left the apartment. I didn't know when he might return.

I remained on the floor, begging God to save me. "Please show me a way out." God nudged me toward Him. These were my first baby steps back to my Savior. Mama tolerated the abuse and ended up in a wheelchair. What did my future hold? What would it take to push me toward a plan of action? Violence. A plan of escape unfolded.

A note concerning the gun: It was always loaded, and he grabbed it quickly. There would have been no time to unload it before pointing it at my head. Did M unload it earlier, or did God cause it to misfire? I know God saved me that day.

The plan: I needed money beyond the few hundred dollars hidden away. I couldn't walk into a hotel with my face swollen and bruised. I gathered only the items most important to me and put them under the bed for quick retrieval. One good thing about a narcissistic sociopath is their lack of awareness of what is important to you. He didn't notice my things had been moved from one place to another within the apartment. After a few days, the swelling went down, and makeup covered the bruises, so I went out. I dreamed of a regular job and erasing my troubled past. I wanted to melt into the world.

On day one of my plan, I had the money I needed. The hotel had a live band and dance floor. It was time for fun. Let's remember, I was twenty-one years old but emotionally sixteen. I did not drink or use drugs. But I loved to dance.

Surprised, I saw my aunt sitting across the room. Next to her was her husband. Yes, the same uncle who sexually abused me on two separate occasions.

We chatted. I told them I had been modeling shoes at the Dallas Market. While true, I did not share that the Dallas Market was a great place for other reasons. I could meet men traveling on business. I did not share the prostitution information, only my desire to leave my current boyfriend. She invited me to live with them. Thank You, Jesus. You did not forget me. Yes, I know, creepy uncle. I reasoned he was no longer interested due to my age. If interest still existed, I could deal with the threat. This living arrangement was a temporary solution. My history had created a streetwise, angry young woman.

DENISE RENKEN

Reflection

I own my decisions. There may be reasons for the decisions, but the choices are mine, and I alone stood before God to answer for them. "M" must stand for his.

Have mercy on me, O God, according to your steadfast love; according to your abundant mercy blot out my transgressions. Wash me thoroughly from my iniquity, and cleanse me from my sin! For I know my transgressions, and my sin is ever before me. Against you, you only, have I sinned and done what is evil in your sight, so that you may be justified in your words and blameless in your judgment. Behold, I was brought forth in iniquity, and in sin did my mother conceive me. Behold, you delight in truth in the inward being, and you teach me wisdom in the secret heart.

Purge me with hyssop, and I shall be clean; wash me, and I shall be whiter than snow. Let me hear joy and gladness; let the bones that you have broken rejoice. Hide your face from my sins, and blot out all my iniquities. Create in me a clean heart, O God, and renew a right spirit within me. Cast me not away from your presence, and take not your Holy Spirit from me. Restore to me the joy of your salvation, and uphold me with a willing spirit.

(Psalm 51:1–12)

Triage Questions

There are many ways we sell ourselves. We sell our desperate hearts to have a mate. Our belief of right and wrong is sold to those who dominate us. God calls us to be servants but not to sell ourselves into servitude. Healthy relationships require give and take, not just give.

Godly counsel checks our belief system with His Word. When we fail to move through life with God, we often sell a piece of ourselves.

1. When you think of the mercy, protection, grace, and forgiveness of God, what comes to mind?

2. How have you seen the power of God in your life?

3. What mental/emotional injuries did you carry into your twenties?

If you're procrastinating, please stop; create your list. While your past is fresh in your mind, begin a list of people who caused you harm. I want you to have time to generate a thorough list. I'll explain more when the time comes to use it.

Next to the offense, list the *damage* done. The event is not as critical to long-term mental/spiritual healing as the *damage* created. Don't forget to include yourself in the list. What decisions have you made that hold regrets for you?

Triage Prayer

Father, there are many ways we sell ourselves. Help us recapture who You created, not what the world has designed. Thank You for gently guiding us to a place of resuscitation. Bless our prayer time with You. Prepare our hearts to recognize everyone and everything we need to release.

In Jesus's name, Amen

Section III

New Beginnings

Chapter 8
Does God Care?

Stage Six: Twenty-One to Twenty-Eight

Young Adulthood

I have mentored women for over thirty-five years and served in a marriage ministry for twenty. Many ladies marry in this age range, so I want to address this part of your heart.

First, to the ladies currently married. You are with your soulmate. By the way, there is no such thing as a soulmate. "We feel a special connection; we have so much in common; we share everything; it's as if we've always known each other." I hear these things from women, dating or newly married.

There is danger in labeling your spouse as your soulmate. We continue to evolve as individuals. The person you married ten years ago is not the same person you are with today. If you lack that wonderful connection you once felt, does that mean you aren't meant to be together? Feelings are real, but I would not make important decisions based on feelings. Whether you rate your marriage a ten or a two, you are married to the right person. Regardless of your current state of marital happiness, God wants you together.

Exception: God does not want you to remain with an abuser. Seek help from your church, family, or friends. It can be challenging to see a way out. Your local domestic abuse agency can help you devise a plan for escape and assistance. God wants the best for your life. That does not include abuse.

Single ladies, when I begin with a new mentee, I listen as they share their woes and disastrous decisions. More than any other decision, they question their marriage decision. Many of these women were Christians when they said yes. Other ladies were far from God when they agreed to marry. What we discover in both instances is a lack of discussion with God. There was a failure to ask God what His desire was for their lives.

It might surprise you to see the similarities between Christian and non-Christian women. The Christian ladies too often believed God would not send someone unless He chose the person for them. So, they don't bother to ask God if he is *the one*. Seldom do they tell me they went to their knees seeking God's counsel. When they prayed about the decision, they only wanted God to confirm a decision already made. They sought a stamp of approval. "If this is not your will, I will walk away" can be a frightening prayer. Walk away from how I feel, the desire for marriage and family on my timing? To want only what is in God's will is a hard prayer. This is no judgment; it is a recognition of the struggle. I cannot claim to have prayed for this when I was young. I did not ask God the first or second time I married. We'll get to my second marriage disaster soon enough.

My non-Christian ladies ask friends and relatives much in the same way Christians ask God. They're not asking for an opinion. They want agreement with the decision. They push the idea. "Doesn't everyone see how happy he makes me?" Whether Christian or non-Christian, blame is cast. If the relationship fails to go as expected, responsibility is often deflected to friends, family, or God. A self-righteous anger toward God may be ignited. Single ladies, please ask God. Find a man who has already dealt with his issues and is active in his relationship with God.

If you are not finding happiness in your marriage, I am beyond sorry for the distress caused by a poorly functioning marriage. I would give you a hug and a tissue if you were here. Then, having determined you are in no physical danger, I would ask you to put separation or divorce on hold. There is help out there for unhealthy marriages. I know the difference between healthy and unhealthy; I've lived it. Place a pause on those big decisions. Discover how God changes hearts and heals mental and spiritual wounds. Allow time for a plan to set boundaries, seek marriage help, and self-help. God can do anything; He can change your life.

We have made strides in the self-help piece of this plan and will continue. Perhaps you have been traumatized and believe you need face-to-face support, but professional counsel is not an option. If you want face-to-face assistance, there are choices. I recommend re:generation, a biblical recovery program offered in many churches in the US. Even if you seek a professional Christian counselor, re:generation is a great addition to their plan. God provides many paths to the redemption of lives. (regenerationrecovery.org)

There is nothing too big for God to carry. Let's continue unveiling issues and inviting Him into the process.

A discussion on marriage help will be in the upcoming chapters. For now, let's work on self-healing as we continue stage six. Use my experiences to bring some of your memories to the forefront. Reflect on how God created you. You were designed to achieve certain strengths in your formative years and later stages. How did events during those years impact your decisions as a young adult, ages eighteen to thirty-five? Did your decision process change for the better? Did you choose margarita buddies as friends? Or did you seek them out for the quality of their lives? In my thirties, I realized my margarita friends were stuck. They were not looking for ways to change the trajectory of their lives. Is it time to adjust your choice of influencers?

Stage six continues; I was twenty-one. No job record for a year made it difficult to find full-time employment. I took two seasonal, Christmas-related part-time retail jobs at Sears and Target. Soon after, I layered an evening server position at a local pizza chain, giving me three part-time jobs. Two months later, the seasonal jobs disappeared, and the pizza job transitioned into a management position. I moved to an apartment.

It was time to tell Papaw, Nannie, and Mama about my divorce. The word divorce weighed five hundred pounds. It represented failure, immorality, and rejection by a decent society. I dreaded the conversation. Their reaction was a mixture of affection for me with disappointment and confusion. Confused because I suppressed the details of why I divorced. My face pleaded with them: *Please don't make me reveal the suffocating shame.* I wept most of the drive back to Dallas.

Dating without God is not a good idea. My internal dialogue: *I'm a hormonal young woman dating young hormonal men. It's normal to date and experience a sexual relationship.* An abortion followed.

I worked twelve to sixteen hours a day to provide for my needs. If I kept the baby, an unknown person would raise the child while I worked. I could not bear the idea of giving a child up for adoption. Fear paralyzed me. I believed the same, or worse, childhood I experienced awaited him or her. Who would be there to rescue? These thoughts drove my decision.

Life is very different when we function without God. We make decisions separated from Him; we serve in the role of god. The result is making regrettable choices. Thirty years would pass before I accepted God's forgiveness and, therefore, forgave myself for the abortion.

Another influence on the decision was Judy, my younger sister. At age sixteen, she gave up a child for adoption. Three days after she gave birth, my grandparents dragged her from the facility. She screamed for the baby she did not want to give away. Her depression gave way to a downward spiral into drugs and alcohol. She surrendered to the abuse of substances. At twenty-seven, her body gave way to death; she was at peace.

After the abortion, my menstrual cycles became sporadic. A multitude of tests revealed I would never have children. Doctors told me it was a result of the abortion and the years of taking too many birth control pills. I thought to myself, *plenty of children need a home. When the day comes for me to become a mom, I will adopt.* For those who struggle with infertility, my heart goes out to you. The depth of your sorrow can be agony. Whether I bore children or adopted them, both methods accomplished the same thing. I was indifferent as to where they came from.

The restaurant job fell apart after two years; it's a long, boring story. I moved back in with my aunt and uncle for two months. Next, I got a job at Texas Instruments (TI) in accounts receivable. I also found a restaurant server position. Most evenings, I worked until closing time. I had two full-time jobs.

At TI, I met David. No one could deny his interest in me. He asked the older ladies in my department, who all adored him, to call him when I left my desk. This allowed him to engineer opportunities to ask me out. He orchestrated reasons to cross paths with me in the corridors of TI.

I didn't want to date and avoided him at every turn. I ducked into the ladies' room, got in a lengthy line at the copy machine, or struck up a conversation with someone else—anything to ward off his advances. He surrendered the chase, formed a frontal attack, and called me at my desk.

I'm about to impress you with my vast worldview analysis of David. He had a stellar work ethic and showed kindness toward children and dogs. He was thoughtful, and we both, at early ages, asked Jesus to be our Savior. That was my checklist of needs.

However, neither of us walked with God. We were in love and lust. After a whirlwind courtship of fourteen weeks, we married. I know, crazy, crazy. When we make decisions without God, what should we expect?

Before our marriage, I shared all my history in an abbreviated fashion. I shared the high-level information because it served no purpose to get into the muddy details. Unwilling to risk someone else telling him and knowing that not all surprises end well, he had a right to know. He listened and replied, "It doesn't matter." I did insist on a church wedding. Marriage should involve God. I love how God continues to pull us toward Him despite our defiance.

David worked one full-time and two part-time jobs. I continued my two full-time jobs. We both knew how to work, and we both wanted an education.

A few months into the marriage, I became pregnant, requiring an adjustment to our finances. We sold my car, quit smoking, and paid off a small credit card debt before the baby's arrival. Eleven months after our wedding, our first baby was born. No one can surprise us the way God does.

We worked on our undergraduate degrees. David pursued his degree full-time in addition to TI. The fall semester would be my last for several years, but David pushed forward.

After a troupe of doctors had previously delivered the sad news that I would never get pregnant, imagine my astonishment with pregnancy number two. If we touched toothbrushes, I got pregnant. David was convinced I deliberately created financial stress and did not speak to me during the second pregnancy. The long, silent car rides back and forth to work became an emotional drain. Old feelings of abandonment surfaced. I volleyed between despair and anger.

The birth of baby number two brought an instant change. David's paternal instincts flipped on; he was elated. But I allowed David's conduct during the pregnancy to drive a wedge into my heart. The failure to process my anger in a manner that identified with God's heart allowed bitterness to take root. Bitterness opens the door for Satan. With great reluctance, I scheduled a procedure for a tubal ligation. There would be no more babies—born or adopted. Growing up, I envisioned several children in my future family. The surgical procedure fueled anger and now resentment. Rather than engaging in an honest conversation, I hid my feelings.

David had been making plans for his MBA. He created a budget for Stanford University, talked with alumni to obtain recommendations, and studied for the GMAT without sharing his plan with me. To say we had communication and conflict-resolution issues is an understatement. You will see this as a common thread through our years together. We functioned as single people, living together in a sexual relationship. David's heart held resentments, too.

This country girl became obsessed with getting our babies a yard for playtime. I pressed for us to get a house. Without God, we find contentment in all the wrong places. On weekends, David did yard work and schoolwork while I cleaned the house, ran errands, and raised our babies. Life's demands and pressures were rising to the surface.

Next, I decided we needed to go to church. God had not forsaken me; the Holy Spirit urged me back to Him. We cleaned up, dressed up, and attended Sunday morning church. In my assessment of Christianity, I had covered the requirements. I took charge of creating the perfect home. What an orchestration of life by a woman who thought herself clever.

When David passed the CPA exam, the focus turned to his MBA. He took a new job with more money, and we bought a second car. This relieved much of the stress related to our one-car life. I had not yet returned to school.

The consistent pattern in my life included control by others. Childhood preparation for good life choices was not in place. My look inward for decisions meant I served in the role of god. I did not ask God what He thought I should do; I didn't know people did things such as ask God. The churches I associated myself with stressed the judgment aspect of Him. God's characteristics seemed harsh, not relational. How could I ask God to forgive me? I didn't know how to forgive myself for my past. How could I ask for God's counsel when my earthly father failed to offer counsel? God did not care about my insignificant life. These and other destructive thoughts limited my growth in Jesus and the restoration of my soul.

1981. David isn't home. He's always home for dinner. It's 11:00 p.m. I'm pacing, frantic. My mind swirls. Is he lying somewhere wounded, unable to seek help? The car must have broken down on the long stretch of interstate leading to our home. At 1:00 a.m., he comes through the door, and I listen to his explanations. My desperate concerns quickly turn to suspicions and then anger. I am twenty-seven, with two babies under three, and David turned our lives upside down.

Satan used this opportunity to set his foothold. I thought, *This can't happen. How did I fail to see the signs? I failed my sweet children. I married a man who was careless with their future.* My mind flooded with these and other questions. I paced. I cried. I spewed anger.

I accused David of the unthinkable; he had been with another woman. He denied it and went to bed. After flipping the combination rollers on his briefcase all night, it opened. I found her name and contact information. I would have made a pit bull of a detective.

The next day, I called her, and we met for lunch. "Please back away; give us time to work on our marriage," I pleaded. "Our babies need their dad." She was harsh in her refusal and wasted no time. She told David about our meeting. Embarrassed and ashamed, he moved out. We divorced. Anger and sadness consumed me; I felt gut-punched.

If you are married or seriously dating, examine these areas of your relationship and rate how you're doing.

Triage Questions

1. **Finances**

    a. Do you agree on how to manage money? How do you work together on financial matters?

    b. Is there debt? How much and from where?

2. **Sexual**

   a. Married—Is there contentment? How would you describe your sexual relationship?

   b. Single—Do you agree with God about purity? If so, what are you doing to remain pure?

3. **Family**

   a. If married, are there boundaries with the in-laws? Is there interference? Describe the relationship with your in-laws.

b. If single, do you agree there should be boundaries with parents and other family members? How might this look?

4. **Communication**

    a. Do you have open, honest discussions? What do you not talk about?

5. **Conflict Resolution**

    a. Do conflicts get resolved?

b. What is your method for working things out? Is everyone in the conflict heard and respected? How does this work?

6. **Children**

a. Is there agreement in parenting? What do you agree with, and what needs some work?

b. If your children are adults, are boundaries in place? What kind?

7. Is there quality time together with spouse, family, friends? What does that look like for you?

8. Do you read the Bible and have a prayer time? Is your faith a top priority? Describe.

Triage Prayer

Father, You know who is suffering a similar reality. Hearts are devastated, health issues loom ahead, monetary provision is daunting, and the loss of loved ones breaks us. Feelings of inadequacy, lack of worth, and loneliness can drive us spiraling. Please gather us into Your arms. Send other women into our lives to listen, love, and counsel. Use my redemption from anguish to help others find their path to You.

In Jesus's name, Amen

Chapter 9
Marriage, Divorce, Marriage

Stage Six: Twenty-Eight to Thirty

Young Adulthood

Divorced, David and I began our new lives. We divided the meager proceeds from the sale of our house. His remorse and the desire to provide for his family drove him to help us. He gave me all the furniture and the household items and provided the maximum child support. All helpful—but empty. The destruction of our family created dark clouds above us.

The children and I moved into the apartment, and I sat on the kitchen floor and cried. Thoughts of David and the other woman sharing a life together shredded my heart. He would not be a part of their daily lives. Other feet played in the yard that had been theirs. I wept for my loneliness, feelings of abandonment, and betrayal. I sobbed a river of tears in shame and sorrow. I believed my children would pay the highest price for my inability to choose wisely in marriage.

Embarrassed by the failed marriage, my church attendance ended. I planted my feet in the world, not with God.

Dating, good grief. My dating adventures included:

Date number one: nice guy, three teenage daughters, no plans to remarry. We enjoyed dinner and conversation, but there was no future.

Date number two: a guy from work. He got crazy drunk and tried in vain to get me into bed; I called a cab.

Date number three: a sweet couple, friends of mine, planned to attend Mardi Gras. Their single friend, who lived in New Orleans, needed a date to the upscale balls. I confess I was intrigued by the possibility of a peek inside that part of society, so I went with him. I paid for my airfare, hotel, and meals; he was to reimburse me for the airfare. Overall, I had a wonderful time. But when sex was a no-go, he refused to reimburse me for airfare.

Airfare was a small price to pay to maintain my purity outside of marriage. God stirred my heart toward His view of life decisions. No, do not be too impressed with the morality. The driver for my morality was not God. My kiddos were positioned on the throne of my heart as *my god*. They were the most important things to me. I would do nothing to bring them shame and disappointment. Whatever is most important in our lives is our god. Our god might be pride, home, kids, career, social media, or alcohol. Ask yourself, "What, or who, is my god?"

David called me the day before he married the other woman, asking me to take him back. Temptation inched me toward yes, but I said no. I wanted the marriage of my imagination, a marriage with trust. With no guarantee of a yes from me, David married her.

An annulment soon ended the marriage. God's pursuit of David drove him to pursue his family. My toxic heart thought David got an annulment because the relationship lost its allure. Regardless of the reason, he wanted us.

David, too, wanted more intimacy than I offered without marriage. In his defense, we lived together before we married the first time. As we began possible marriage discussions, I brought the topic of church to the forefront. I convinced David that our family needed to go to church, so he agreed. If David had initiated our return to church, it would have indicated a *possible* heart change toward God. David agreed, and Sunday attendance began. Convinced the perfect plan was in place, we asked the pastor to marry us in his office.

An interesting side note: Before we remarried, one of the women in a leadership position at the church came to visit me at home. An intervention unfolded. She implored me not to remarry David. "You're attractive and will easily find someone else to help rear the children." Please, ladies, be careful of the counsel you receive. The moment advice reflects the world's ways, not God's, remove yourself. A biblical counsel would have suggested, "Please seek professional help before you remarry," rather than closing the door to the possibility of what God can do.

David's promise to attend church and fidelity gave me peace to remarry. Our divorce to remarriage had taken just eight months. We bought a new home to start our perfect life. I became a stay-at-home mom and supplemented our income by selling Tupperware and Avon products. And I cared for a few children part-time to fill the financial gap. David kept his word, attending church, but stopped after six months.

> For godly grief produces a repentance that leads
> to salvation without regret, whereas worldly
> grief produces death.
> (2 Corinthians 7:10)

The *other woman* became a regular pattern in our marriage. I pretended not to know. My struggle with conflict avoidance can be linked to an excess of childhood issues. Today, if I cannot see a path to resolution, my temptation is to avoid the conflict. However, I *struggle well,* meaning I recognize I have an issue but allow God's view to take control of the matter. There is value in the reconciliation of conflict when executed biblically. I understand improvement comes as I seek His ways, not mine. More on the topic of conflict later.

Volumes of women passed through our lives. I was surprised when I finally discovered the number. I searched twelve-step programs and listened to relatives' and friends' recommendations while drowning in a sea of despair.

Triage Prayer

Father, give us the courage to transfer our past and present wounds to You. Calm our anxious hearts. You know the condition of our relationships. Guide us to know when to pause desperate decisions such as divorce. We need time to heal and absorb your wisdom. We want to make better life decisions. Ease the damage to our souls, allowing us to see life challenges with clarity for our next steps.

In Jesus's name, Amen

Section IV

The Path to Healing

Chapter 10
God Draws Us to Him

> **Completion of Stage Six: Thirty to Thirty-five**

Young Adulthood

In 1985, David's career moved us to Raleigh, NC. Raleigh mimicked a small-town culture. Strangers greeted me with a warm hello that spoke of a long friendship. Grocery store conversations shared the details of current life events. Exiting a parking lot into traffic was met with a driver's motions for you to get in front of them. No one was treated as an outsider or an inconvenience. The experience was precious to me, a young woman who was far from family and friends.

North Carolina is a beautiful state. "Welcome home," the breeze whispered. Pine trees swayed, and red clay soil spoke the language of an East Texas landscape. My soul smiled.

Cell phones, home computers, and email access did not exist in 1985. The thirteen hundred miles from family and friends eliminated contact with those I left behind. Within a month, David added another woman into his world. He stopped any attempt to hide the betrayal. He left early, before the kids got up, and returned late in the evening or the early morning hours of the next day. I functioned as a single mom—a lonely, heartbroken woman struggling to be strong for my children.

I'm sure my family and the people who knew me had good intentions, but they said some pretty crazy things about the cause of the infidelity:

1. Financial stress. But David's increase in pay with the relocation freed us of financial stress.

2. Kids' toys were scattered. But the house was always a showplace by the end of the day.

3. Not enough sex with me. Seriously? At least five times a week. Yes, with him away so often, it might seem impossible. I'm going to assume you do not want to know the details of how he managed to work our sex life into his schedule.

4. My weight. Good grief—5-foot 3 inch, and 115 pounds. I no longer thought 110 pounds would solve the issue.

5. Not praising him enough. Uh-huh, right.

The list went on. The general message from everyone laid the infidelity on my shoulders to fix. Oppressive voices from those who live by the world's wisdom can feed hopelessness. I heard the extremes, from blaming me to religious legalism dictating there was never a reason to divorce. No one approached me with, "Let me share how God values you." "What does God want for your heart?" "Let's look at some boundaries to put in place as you move through your marriage."

Understanding the true state of my marriage pounded me like a ton of bricks. My mind swam as I realized I couldn't fix our marriage, and he didn't care. Unable to form a plan, I robotically moved through the first few months in Raleigh. Loneliness set up residence. Sexual fantasies about other men took root.

For years, I had belittled myself, believing I was the problem. I knew I needed to work on myself but now realized nothing warranted his choices. My eyes opened to the seriousness of my situation—I was in big, *big* trouble.

The Holy Spirit was drawing me to Him. He whispered, "Without David's restoration with God, your marriage has no hope." *No hope*. No hope is a dreadful, shadowy pit.

Why did I decide to remain married, you ask?

1. **My history.** Examining my past identifies a struggle with *codependency* issues. WebMD identifies the following as signs of codependency:[1]

    a. Low self-esteem
    b. Trouble identifying our own emotions
    c. Trouble making decisions
    d. The desire to care for others
    e. Desire to feel important to someone

I stepped away from codependency in small ways. Discovering my value to God helped me examine *my* wants and needs.

I went back to college, took martial arts, and became active in church. Now, when codependency creeps into my life, I catch myself quickly and redirect my view to God.

2. **I knew the pain of growing up without a father.** That was not going to be my children's future. My view of the road ahead of family gatherings, vacations, weddings, and grandchildren became clear. I wanted a unified family.

3. **My fears.** If I divorced, I would live in an unsafe part of town. My insufficient education led to visions of hardship. I viewed poverty with an indescribable fear. Anxiety about my children being lured into gang involvement, violence, substance abuse, and prison paralyzed me. These scenarios play out in real life, not just on television.

4. **My walk with God.** The Bible states God hates divorce (Malachi 2:16). Although God allows exceptions, it does not change the fact that He *hates* divorce. When I prayed about divorce, I received no indication God wanted me to take that step. He made other things clear to me but not divorce. I was convinced God did not want me to surrender the marriage to Satan. Did I accurately discern God's intent? Perhaps. Perhaps not.

Without the support of family and friends nearby, I began to lean more on God. He loved me so much that He removed my harmful influencers, the folks not yet searching for God's view of living.

Feelings of loneliness and depression flooded me. God leaned into me when I didn't know how to lean into Him. I asked myself, "If I am God's daughter, what does it mean? How do I become worthy to be called His?" An uphill journey lay ahead. My multitude of regrets and shame was overpowering.

Interestingly, the separation from family and the reality of my marriage drove me toward a path of healing mentally and spiritually. It was in my search for a solution that I encountered Erikson's life stage tools. Understanding my foundational childhood issues provided a path forward of focused, specific prayers for God's intervention.

The starting place was easy. I needed to take my children and myself to church, read the Bible daily, and pray. For the first time, I began in earnest to know Him. He knew my sins, my damaged psyche, my heartache. He had caught every tear. Centered on God and my restoration, He straightened my path. I was not able to step to the left or the right. As I worked on myself, I placed other life changes on hold, including divorce. My emotional emptiness created a weakness. This weakened condition would not allow me to target both myself and the marriage. I brought myself to the forefront. Finding godly women for counsel took time and effort, so the beginning of the path would be accomplished with just God and me.

Reflection

I must be careful. I tend to seclude myself, not an appropriate life pattern.

> *Whoever isolates himself seeks his desire; he breaks out against all sound judgment. A fool takes no pleasure in understanding, but only in expressing his opinion.*
> *(Proverbs 18:1–2)*

My prayer life has evolved. Today it is a quest for God's will in my life. Early in the prayer process, I prayed for the sweet, tender things we women pray for. Then, there were the times I prayed for a Mack truck to run over David. "Please, God, he is the greatest source of destruction in our lives; just take him out." I admit I'm not proud of that prayer before the throne of Almighty God. There were times when my anger proved stronger than my compassion. The Mack truck prayer only lasted a couple of weeks before God took me to Mark 11:25—"And whenever you stand praying, forgive, if you have anything against anyone, so that your Father also who is in heaven may forgive you your trespasses."

The Holy Spirit continued convicting me to work on my sins and not focus on David's. Did I get angry at times? Yes. Did I cry a river of tears? Yes. But my heart was following Jesus most of the time.

It's all right for a new Christian to take small steps to learn how to be God's child. It takes discipline to read His Word daily. There is a richness in sitting quietly as you read your Bible. The Holy Spirit will reach into your soul's recesses to both convict and comfort you. Prayers that honor God come from a heart that is repaired or in the process of healing. Time and commitment make these things more consistent.

We were in Raleigh for five years. God used Erikson to identify my wounds and then repaired my damaged soul. Though David's list of women grew, these are a few items God pressed into my heart throughout those years:

— **Forgiveness stops the transition of anger into bitterness.** Forgive, not condone, but forgive daily, often moment by moment. If we sit in anger, it evolves into bitterness and will allow a path for Satan to taint our discernment.

> Blessed is the man who remains steadfast under trial, for when he has stood the test he will receive the crown of life, which God has promised to those who love him. Let no one say when he is tempted, "I am being tempted by God," for God cannot be tempted with evil, and he tempts no one. But each person is tempted when he is lured and enticed

> by his own desire. Then desire when it has
> conceived gives birth to sin, and sin when it is
> fully grown brings forth death.
> (James 1:12–15)

— **Love myself.** Stop comparing myself to others. I was assessing my life based on other women—my looks, possessions, children, marriage, and education. Comparisons contaminated the perception of *my* worth before the God who created me in His image.

God loves me and wants the best for my life. Seeking His counsel brings me peace. How wonderful to talk with someone without an agenda. He wants to help me, and He does not compare me to anyone.

> You shall not covet your neighbor's house; you
> shall not covet your neighbor's wife, or his
> male servant, or his female servant, or his ox,
> or his donkey, or anything that is your neighbor's.
> (Exodus 20:17)

— **Sisters in Christ press God's truth into my life.** Choose friends with God's wisdom. At first, I closed the deepest personal areas of my life to women walking without God. I intentionally sought counsel from people of God, as I needed guidance to ensure my life was aligned with His plan. After God's healing, I learned to share areas of my life with women who were not walking well without seeking their advice.

> But he replied to the man who told him, "Who is my mother, and who are my brothers?" And stretching out his hand toward his disciples, he said, "Here are my mother and my brothers! For whoever does the will of my Father in heaven is my brother and sister and mother.
> (Matthew 12:48–50)

My friends committed themselves to respecting their husbands. This does not mean we resembled doormats. We made the decision not to make fun of men in general.

Examples included avoiding commercials and TV programs that put men down in the name of humor, and we did not roll our eyes at our husbands.

I still struggle with my tone of voice, but I have improved. Thank You, Holy Spirit. You care enough to convict me and exhibit patience during moments of failure.

— God commanded me to respect my husband. Oh my, this was a tough one. Anger rose to argue with God, but my heart followed Jesus. I ask Him, "How do I respect this man who is destroying our family?"

We step into obedience to God through repentance. Repentance is a changing of our minds and soul. It is recognition that we are wrong, and God is right. My action of respecting David did not indicate I *felt* respect.

Agreeing with God, led me to focus on things I could respect about David. He financially sustained us, did not gamble, did not use drugs, and did not drink to excess. He supported my decisions concerning what was best for me and our children. He attended their practices/games and, sometimes, coached them. He had a strong work ethic and never physically abused us. When the kids complained about church attendance, he said, "Your mother is right, go to church."

> This mystery is profound, and I am saying that it refers to Christ and the church. However, let each one of you love his wife as himself, and let the wife see that she respects her husband.
> (Ephesians 5:32,33)

— **Pray without ceasing.** In the car, while cleaning the house, and while doing yard work, I pray regularly.

> Rejoice always, pray without ceasing, give thanks in all circumstances; for this is the will of God in Christ Jesus for you.
> (1 Thessalonians 5:16–18)

— **Read His Word.** We speak to God through prayer. He speaks to us through His Word and convictions of the Holy Spirit. A healthy relationship is not one-sided. I need His voice to pierce the chaos of my life. I read daily.

> You shall therefore lay up these words of mine in
> your heart and in your soul, and you shall bind
> them as a sign on your hand, and they shall
> be as frontlets between your eyes. You shall
> teach them to your children, talking of them
> when you are sitting in your house, and when
> you are walking by the way, and when you lie
> down, and when you rise. You shall write them
> on the doorposts of your house and
> on your gates.
> (Deuteronomy 11:18–20)

— God has a sense of humor and wisdom beyond our feeble understanding.

Given my history, I did not know where to start to change my life. I wanted to reflect a daughter of God. My sins were enemies on a battlefield, overwhelming me. Cross-legged, Bible on my lap, I stared at the wall across from me. Please, God, triage my brokenness. Sort this mental chaos so I know which sin to remove first. Use Erikson's process and Your wisdom to guide me. I sat weeping, shattered, in need of a Savior.

My custom was to fight battles alone. But God's way of fighting was different. I prayed, read my Bible, and asked God to guide me on how to make life changes. The Holy Spirit convicted me to stop lying. When I opened my eyes from prayer, I said, " I am *not* a liar. You can ask anyone who knows me. They might say I need to work on many things but will agree I am *not* a liar. There are a multitude of things I'm doing wrong. Seriously, this is where You want me to start?"

Research via the dictionary revealed lying as any attempt to deceive. I was a liar. He was right. Three years later, I had rid myself of all lying. What a chore to speak the truth when someone asks you about the crazy thing they just did to their hair. God has a profound sense of humor. It taught me to slow down, to speak truth in love. Of course, while I was working on the truth issue, He rebuilt other broken pieces of my soul. I would love to say I never argued with God again, but it would be a lie.

> Whoever gets sense loves his own soul; he
> who keeps understanding will discover good.
> A false witness will not go unpunished,
> and he who breathes out lies will perish.
> (Proverbs 19:8–10)

— **Trust the Holy Spirit.** He convicts us, tenderly directs us on our path, and, on our behalf, carries unspoken prayers to God. Stop trying to be the Holy Spirit for yourself, your spouse, and others to point out sin. It is not my job to decide what others need to work on; it is the Holy Spirit's job to convict. If you asked anyone what I needed to work on first, no one close to me would have said lying, but the Holy Spirit chose it. Allow time and space for the Holy Spirit to work *His* will.

Despite my brokenness, God sent women for me to mentor. Women around me noticed the changes in my attitude and wanted to know what I was doing. The primary changes from the above list, reflect God's move of my spirit for those years and years to come. God knew the best use of my energies for mental and spiritual growth. I was in the eye of David's storm established by his serial affairs.

One woman phoned me at home to share the sexual things they enjoyed together. She told me about the restaurants and movies they shared. I found gifts for other women hidden in the trunk of his car or on top of our bookcases.

I came across beautiful packages in his truck because I was snooping. I studied the packages to determine how to open and rewrap them and leave no trace. I took them into the house. David was upstairs sleeping; it was 3 a.m. One ribbon at a time, I carefully took them apart. Opened, I sprinkled motor oil inside before I returned them to their pristine status. Just making sure we all understand, I was not walking with God well every moment of every day.

We each are on a separate path with God. It can be easy to make sinful choices if we lack a close relationship with Him. In the first couple of years in Raleigh, one of my coping mechanisms involved overcrowding my schedule. I didn't want time to dwell on the other women. Commitments: Block captain in our neighborhood, PTA treasurer, and Sunday school teacher in my youngest child's class, taking the kids' team sports practices/games, doing martial arts along with the kids, worked part-time, attended classes at North Carolina State, taking care of our home and the yard work, led an exercise class for the elderly and homeroom assistant in my older child's class. I hit overload and backed away from most of these. God will allow us to run crazy until we get exhausted and run to Him.

Projecting the image of a happy home consumed much of my time. The primary reason for this camouflage was to protect the kids. Moms are protective when deciding who their children spend time with, and I didn't want my children shunned. I worked hard on image control. The priorities we set without asking God.

On a November night in 1988, our home took a direct hit from an F4 tornado. It was 1:00 a.m. when it developed over our neighborhood, coming straight down with little warning. I don't know how to describe the level of devastation an F4 creates. I will say it attracts the worst people in the form of looters and the best strangers who show up to help. However, this is not a story of our F4 experience. I mention it because I am thankful David was home. It was typical for him to be out later than 1:00 a.m. I am grateful not just for us but for David's sake. God spared David the regret of not being with us to serve as the protector of his family. It is a sweet moment of God's grace for David. Thank You, Father, for our lives. Some did not survive.

The Raleigh years ended, but nothing in the marriage changed. I continued to be a wife, including regular sexual activity with David. I grew in my relationship with Jesus and continued using Erikson's analysis.

Reflection

Father, thank You for using my meager and inadequate attempts to draw my children to You. It blesses me to see who they are today.

Train up a child in the way he should go;
even when he is old, he will not depart from it.
(Proverbs 22:6)

Triage Prayer

Father, we sit in the quiet, we ask the Holy Spirit to convict us of the needed changes in our lives. Help us hear Your desire for us. Create discernment and courage to make good choices.

In Jesus's name, Amen

Chapter 11
Going Home

In 1988, Mama moved into a nursing facility, and Papaw passed away the next year. David's next career promotion required a transfer to a different city. He pushed Nortel to relocate us back to Texas, for my sake. I needed to get back before I lost more pieces of my family. I think it's appropriate to pause here and recognize David's actions. There were times when he was the kind and thoughtful man I married the first time.

By 1990, we were back in the Dallas area. David had another woman within a month. My prayers still asked God to provide direction and His continued healing of my heart. These prayers also included, "Please make David into the husband and father he should be."

I injured my back the week we moved into the house, and all exercise halted. I had to reduce exercise to only walking the dog. My failure to make dietary adjustments led to weight piling on.

Most days, I would drop the kiddos off at school and head to school myself. I increased my class schedule, pushing myself to complete my undergraduate degree in accounting. Later, I would go on to complete an MBA and CPA. The CPA governing body performs a criminal background check on candidates. I hired an attorney before attacking the arduous task of conquering the CPA exam. The attorney had my arrest for prostitution expunged from the records. A huge weight lifted. No one would ever need to know. God's humor is well placed as I author this book to tell all.

I received notification that attendants at the nursing home discovered Mama slumped over her large-print Bible. She had gone to the Lord. Nannie passed the next year. Thank you again, David, for insisting we relocate back to Texas. It gave me time with family before their passing.

My anguish over the weight gain was already dragging me into a pit of despair. With Mama and Nannie gone, a different emptiness settled over me. Depression hovered. My occasional struggle with depression and suicidal thoughts reemerged. Now tentacles of hopelessness, with my weight gain and the loss of loved ones, intertwined into a desire to isolate. I withdrew into myself, similar to an internal fetal position. God and I had fought this battle before and won.

Knowing I did not require medication, and God could get me through anything, I became diligent in recognizing the early signs of a downward spiral. The downward spiral, for me, was Satan pushing his way into my internal dialogue. He told me, "You don't matter. You're a fat failure as a wife and mother." God's wisdom whispered, "The negative thoughts in your mind could never come from me. You are my daughter, wonderfully made and loved."

I learned to discern these thoughts were not from God, which meant they must come from Satan. Only he would want me to feel bad about myself, to think I had no value. He wanted me to feel defeated, betrayed, and abandoned. He would say things like, "What you have will be all life will ever offer you." God would never press those things into my mind and heart. Recognizing the difference in messaging gave me power—the power to tell Satan he had no place in my life, my home, my children's lives, or David's life. The Holy Spirit lived in my heart. That's power. I took my Bible from room to room, read His Word, and commanded Satan's forces to leave. I received less frequent visits from darkness. Why was I so vulnerable to the stresses of weight gain and family loss?

One metaphor rings true with me about why this could be. Imagine your kitchen sink. You've inserted a stopper and turned on the faucet. Sludge comes from the faucet, filling the sink. In vain, you try to turn it off, and before the catastrophe of overflow strikes, you pull the stopper and allow the sink to drain. The faucet is our mind and soul during trauma; the sludge is the damage in need of release. Both need attention.

When we find ourselves in overwhelming situations, we need to turn the faucet off when possible. Boundaries are needed, and this might mean certain people need to be temporarily separated or permanently removed from our lives. Regardless, the stopper must be released.

David represented the faucet I did not turn off, the daily trauma. I had pulled the stopper while in Raleigh. My release mechanism was God and Erikson. Most of the permanent healing was related to my childhood years. Soul repair and my growth with God changed how I made many decisions. I accepted God's value of me. I was committed to seeing life through His lens. My faucet continued to bear down on me.

Reflection

Husbands are unaware of the damage they do when they abandon their wives on the battlefield. We battle the forces of evil every day. If a commander abandoned his troops on the battlefield, society would deem it appalling. But the world around us wants to assess blame for a failed marriage rather than acknowledge the forces of evil in play.

> *Husbands, love your wives, as Christ loved the church and gave himself up for her, that he might sanctify her, having cleansed her by the washing of water with the word, so that he might present the church to himself in splendor, without spot or wrinkle or any such thing, that she might be holy and without blemish. In the same way, husbands should love their wives as their own bodies. He who loves his wife loves himself.*
> *(Ephesians 5:25–28)*

My kids approached their teen years, and I became the mom who yelled. Yes, I had raised my voice before these years arrived, but it was rare. Raising our voices in frustration or anger does not honor God. A God-centered spirit and a repaired mind will lead to godly parenting. If I had not been on the path of mental repair, I likely would have smacked one or both of them during puberty. Teen behavior lifted the top off the powder keg of anger in my heart.

The groundwork done in the Raleigh years springboarded me to the next level of mental health. I found a Christian psychologist and spent eighteen months delving into my past and current issues. In addition to his counseling services, he held Saturday seminars on parenting. The seminar changed my skill set and how I approached my teenagers.

I continued utilizing Erikson's models to reveal injuries. God's Word and prayer were like a salve that layered onto the wounds. The Balm of Gilead poured on my soul. My perception of the world around me and the people in it shifted positively. I found power in forgiveness that gently removed the scabs of old injuries. God was continuing to restore me, His daughter. Healing does not mean we forget. Repair transfers the grief, pain, and bitterness to God. It becomes a floating puff of smoke carried away in the gentle breezes of a Savior.

During my seasons of life, I have shifted my prayer time from morning to evening to afternoon. One morning, after taking my teens to school, my time in the Word led me to verses that broke my heart and forever altered the trajectory of my life:

"That the God of our Lord Jesus Christ, the Father of glory, may give you the Spirit of wisdom and of revelation in the knowledge of him, having the eyes of your hearts enlightened, that you may know what is the hope to which he has called you, what are the riches of his glorious inheritance in the saints" (Ephesians 1:17–18).

And just like that, I realized David was more than my husband; he was my brother in Christ and had lost his way. Putting a mirror to my face, God asked, "Do you recall a time when you lost your way too?" Right then, I gave up my right to have the husband I wanted. My concern now became David's state before the throne of God. For many years following, I prayed this passage for David and over him as he slept. Funny side note: One night, he woke up as I prayed over him. Startled, he said, "What are you doing? Stop it, that's creepy." I just waited for him to go back to sleep and continued my prayer for him.

Reflection

God linked Ephesians 1:17–18 to the passages below. These verses made me question how selfish I would be not to want the absolute best of God's blessings for David.

TRIAGE

Thus says the Lord:
"Cursed is the man who trusts in man
and makes flesh his strength,
whose heart turns away from the Lord.
He is like a shrub in the desert,
and shall not see any good come.
He shall dwell in the parched places of the
wilderness, in an uninhabited salt land.
"Blessed is the man who trusts in the Lord,
whose trust is the Lord.
He is like a tree planted by water,
that sends out its roots by the stream,
and does not fear when heat comes,
for its leaves remain green,
and is not anxious in the year of drought,
for it does not cease to bear fruit."

The heart is deceitful above all things,
and desperately sick;
who can understand it?
"I the Lord search the heart
and test the mind,
to give every man according to his ways,
according to the fruit of his deeds."
(Jeremiah 17:5–10)

With my undergraduate degree accomplished, I took a position with a communications company. I began my MBA work. David's career continued to advance along with our income.

The energy to make good marital decisions still did not exist. I prayed and trusted God would tell me what to do and when. While putting away laundry, I discovered a business card for an attorney in David's drawer. Digging deeper through his things, I found personal notes and cards from other women. You might wonder why I had not discovered these items earlier. My days of toxicity searching his car and other things had passed. From my perspective, what was the point? I knew what he was doing. I could not control David, only my responses and my mental health.

I read the notes. One of the women was someone I considered a close friend. The relationship had drifted when she moved three hours away, but we were friends, or so I thought. I remembered a time when she visited me, staying in my home for several days. This visit aligned with the same time they were having their affair. I was stunned. Grief and anger took control.

David came home to an angry, determined woman. I initiated and escalated an argument that was one for the ages. Every bottled-up frustration surfaced. Soon after, I hired my own attorney. David moved to an apartment. His path to redemption was underway but invisible to me. When you think things could not get worse, they often do.

A month later, David came by, hoping to talk to our kids, but they avoided him. It is our tradition to decorate for Christmas the Friday after Thanksgiving. David helped decorate the tree, I decorated the mantle, and Larnelle Harris sang "Oh Holy Night" in the background. What a family photo. The doorbell rang.

Behind my front door stood David's latest woman. Angered that he had ended the relationship, she brought the items he had left at her place. She handed me the items in a plastic bag, spewed her opinions of David, turned, and walked to her car. I held it together while she vented and watched her walk away. The door closed to find David staring at me wide-eyed, his face drained of all blood, frozen in his tracks. Gathering himself, he tried to console my unleashed sobs. I whirled my angry tone toward him. "Get out. Never touch me again. Leave and never return to this home." *Home.* Who was I fooling?

Five minutes before she came, my eldest left the house via that same door. And ten minutes after she left, my youngest came home through that door. Neither of them was home during the woman's visit, spared of forever having the encounter pressed into their memory. Thank You, God.

Reflection

Thank You, Father, for the coverage of protection. David did not father children with any other women. Thank You for protecting me from STDs. Thank You for pressing into my heart I am Yours and forgiven. Thank You for letting me know there is nothing You cannot carry me through.

> *Therefore, my beloved brothers, be steadfast, immovable, always abounding in the work of the Lord, knowing that in the Lord your labor is not in vain.*
> *(1 Corinthians 15:58)*

David went back to his apartment. I was no longer communicating with him. I began a month of tears, beseeching God to show me His will. The decision for the second divorce positioned itself in front of me. Had I come this far only to have God end it? *Surely not*, I thought. I spent so many years determined not to surrender the marriage. God hates divorce, right? However, this time when I prayed, the Holy Spirit urged me to end the marriage. Although David was the first to consult an attorney, he did not want the divorce finalized. After agonizing in prayer, I believed God wanted me to put the last nail into the coffin, to bury the marriage. I signed the papers, and we divorced, yes, again.

Weeks stretched into months. For the first time, David respected my boundaries. Divorce is a shredding, a tearing process of lives—a painful, gut-wrenching path I recommend to no one. "Please, God, will my life forever be held captive by grief and heartache?" Empty, barely able to function with life's demands, I spent hours with God. Cross-legged on my sofa, Bible on my lap, I read through tear-filled eyes. I refused to take a step without the peace of knowing God's direction.

The history of our separations reflected David saying things like, "I said I'm sorry, why can't we just move on? When are you going to get over this?" The emails he sent after I demanded he leave were different. Those emails offered no apologies or pleas for reconciliation. They echoed a broken man, sharing what he was reading in his Bible and how it moved his heart. I might have deleted the emails without ever reading them. Or I might have read them but never answered. David had no expectations.

Over time, I began to believe David was responding to his heart, directed by the Holy Spirit. No two-way communication existed between us. My aspiration for a pleasant relationship to allow us to co-parent seemed reasonable. One Sunday afternoon, with opera tickets in hand, my friend called to cancel. I don't recall why she couldn't go; it must not be important to the story other than God opened a door.

I called David and invited him to join me at the opera. David was not a fan, but I loved the opera. His answer of yes let me know he wanted time with me. The performance was, shall we say, less than stellar. Along with a third of the audience, we left during the first intermission. We began to talk. Not daily, but often.

The tone of dialogue evolved at a rapid pace. David once again was pursuing me. I knew a proposal was imminent. I prayed, "God, I do not want to decide on anything without You at the center of it. You would never want me to risk suffering again by marrying David." In reality, I had already made my decision not to remarry him. I only pretended to ask God. It's amusing how we can see things more clearly in retrospect. The Holy Spirit responded, "Say yes." I said to God *aloud*, "I'm sure I didn't ask clearly, so I'll be back tomorrow to chat." I laugh at my absurdity. Each time I asked God, the Holy Spirit said yes, marry him. I went back and forth with God on this for a while.

It was a warm Texas spring day. Time expended on the details of makeup and hair was behind me. The pale pink suit rested tenderly smoothed across the bed for the afternoon occasion. I stared at it, knowing it would help me look my best. I'd feel pretty, which was not a common thought I had about myself.

After the ceremony, we would have lunch with a few close friends. Thinking of the details of the upcoming event had kept anxiety to a minimum. Only God could calm my anxious heart. I had so many conversations with Him about this decision. No one agreed with what I was about to do, but God kept urging me forward. Peace filled me as I trusted Him to carry me through the chaos of uncertainty. God is an expert in chaos. He created an entire universe from chaos. I decided to trust Him, not the world. I would step off a cliff and trust God to catch me as I free-fell. I was about to marry David for a third time.

My primary goal was to find ways to allow God to continue the miracle of repair to my heart. Much of the healing work God had done for me was life-impacting. My approach to decisions, setting boundaries with family and friends where needed, and my anger issues were all vastly improved. But when you experience continued emotional beatings, those wounds can surface as raw. Emotionally, I had zero to offer. Good news, our God can do anything. He can part seas to dry land and raise people from the dead. Our God can do anything.

With the Lord telling me to say yes, I trusted Him. I married David.

Triage Prayer

Father, thank You for Your perfect timing. You encouraged me to say yes yet left me partly broken. My brokenness gave David a view of the consequences of betrayal. Thank You for Your power in our lives. Thank You for shepherding our forgiveness and the restoration of trust. Press into women's hearts to trust You and Your timing.

In Jesus's name, Amen.

Section V

Restoration

Chapter 12
Triage Heart Repair

What Forgiveness Is and Is Not

Buried in the rubble of my life, I appealed to God to restore my heart. Knowing the connective thread of restoration and forgiveness was critical, it was time to forgive. The recognition of my need for a more thorough process toward forgiveness began when *the woman* came to my house with David's things.

Branded with the word "victim," first by others, then myself, I asked God, "Is this all You planned for my life? What happened to the little girl You created me to be? A girl undamaged, destined to be a woman of God? Father, help me find a path of *complete* forgiveness. Help me find myself."

Yes, growth in my relationship with God included many years on a consistent path of forgiveness. But there are multiple layers when it comes to full forgiveness. Unforgiveness shackles you to the damage, and I didn't want to be in bondage anymore. Prayers for a heart of forgiveness intertwined with my quiet time. My achievement of forgiving David, at this point, was related only to surface-level issues of infidelity. God already granted the healing of childhood damage and restoration, which gave me the courage and insight to move forward.

God stripped away the power of evil that dared come near me. The grief, self-pity, and certainty of His next steps required my full attention. God returned me to clay. He was about to rebuild a new woman, one who was restored. The time to get serious about forgiveness was at hand. Erikson's approach to the chronological division of life served me well, and I segmented my forgiveness plan into increments of ten years. Focus on the people who impacted my life became manageable.

My Triage Plan

I began with a tourniquet of sorts to stop the bleeding of new injuries so I could triage the more serious past wounds. The Holy Spirit guided me to reassess my *expectations* of people. This insight forged a lifetime pattern toward forgiveness in my life. For example, parents should provide their children with unconditional love and protection. They may or may not deliver on these expectations, but it is *appropriate* to expect trustworthy and protective parents.

Let's sit here for a moment and discuss righteous anger. Jesus exhibited righteous anger when He flipped over the tables in the temple and shared His opinion of their ungodly actions. But you never read about it again. He did not grumble on and on about it. It did not fester in His heart. We can have righteous anger with those we should be able to depend on. Parents are only one example.

Was my anger toward David's breach of trust righteous? Absolutely. Did it give me license to allow bitterness in my heart? No. Without David following God, I should have had zero expectations of long-term changes.

Inappropriate expectations are those we form about people not close to us. No personal relationship exists. We should have minimum expectations for people in traffic, the grocery store, school, and work. Think about the craziness of folks in traffic. We witness foul sign language and screams of obscenities. When someone cuts us off in traffic, we decide if anger will be our response. No one forces us to react unpleasantly. How we respond to the world reflects the condition of our hearts. Adjusting my expectations has been a life-changer. If I expect little to nothing, there is nothing to feed my anger and nothing to forgive. It keeps a large section of my heart well protected. Proverbs 4:23 urges us to guard our hearts, for from them flow the springs of life. I'm not surprised when someone acts crazy in traffic, only mildly irritated. There is no wound and, therefore, no soul damage.

The group of *appropriate* expectations is more challenging. These are family, friends, and other Christians. My hopes for this group are higher. The injury received hits harder. My reset for forgiving Christians came from God's perspective. Christians are not perfect humans. I disappoint those close to me; my conduct and attitude do not always display the Spirit of God. Christians offer grace, just as our Lord offers grace. My failures do not permit me to ignore my call to become Christ-like. Have I been so disappointed or wounded by a fellow Christian that it required processing the damage with God? Yes. But it is rare.

Family and friends: Relationships we are not prepared to permanently eliminate may need boundaries. These boundaries reset the relationship in a way that protects the heart. Books on boundaries are available if you need a more thorough plan.

These realignments of expectations served as a tourniquet for ongoing wounds. Living in a continuous state of grace allowed me to focus on forgiving past harms and move forward with a plan for deeper healing.

Erikson's life stages method triaged and sorted my wounds. It brought events to the surface and allowed me to analyze the damage caused by the event. Prayer brought a thorough understanding of how God's view of forgiveness was necessary to complete the healing process.

Again, forgiveness is not a pardon of the trespass. We forgive the resulting damage caused by the event. Forgiveness releases the need for apologies, justice, punishment, and confession and recognizes the harm. It respects that God will save/forgive folks or put them where He deems proper. My heart holds no harshness or vindictiveness.

Please do not misunderstand. This process does not pray for God to render His hand of justice on anyone. I relinquish my right to perceived justice, hoping that God will pull them to Himself in a spirit of repentance and salvation. I want everyone to repent, accept Jesus as Lord, and spend eternity in heaven, knowing a selfish heart needs healing. Like Jesus, we pray for our enemies: "But I say to you, Love your enemies and pray for those who persecute you" (Matthew 5:44). When I understood the state of my enemies before God, I went to my knees in prayer.

> "Their throat is an open grave;
> they use their tongues to deceive."
> "The venom of asps is under their lips."
> "Their mouth is full of curses and bitterness."
> "Their feet are swift to shed blood;
> in their paths are ruin and misery,
> and the way of peace they have not known."
> "There is no fear of God before their eyes."
> (Romans 3:13–18)

What Forgiveness Is Not

As we dig more into the concept of forgiveness, it's important to understand what it is and what it is not. Let's start with what forgiveness is not and what it doesn't do.

1. Forgiveness does not condone what occurred nor the things neglected. I do not excuse my uncle's sexual conduct against me nor the failure of others to protect me. And I don't brush aside my sins against myself and others.

2. Forgiveness does not establish trust. Children step into confidence because they lack the discernment to make such evaluations. They are at the mercy of those in authority who decide who and what to trust.

Adults view things through the eyes of experience. Dark alleys, underground parking garages, and boats in ill-repair signal caution.

People who have breached our trust require us to keep a keen eye on them, and we listen for God's wisdom. Trust is established over time with proven change.

When we share a confidence with a friend or a relative, and that confidence is broken, will we readily share with them again? No. Even when trust is broken, we must forgive. The restoration of trust should be earned, though. (I'll explain how and why David regained my trust later.)

3. Forgiveness is not restoration. God is a god of restoration. Otherwise, Jesus's sacrifice would not have been required. He died for the possibility of a restored relationship with us. Where possible, God wants relationships restored. We are also called to guard our hearts and be discerning. I forgave "M," but it would be ridiculous to rebuild the relationship. I want God to cleanse my heart of the toxic damage inflicted as I move through forgiveness.

What Forgiveness Is

Now let's start with what forgiveness is and what it does. In John 8:7, Jesus said, "Let him who is without sin among you be the first to throw a stone at her." None of us are without sin, so we need to lay down our stones and our need to see the other person suffer for theirs. There are two steps we can take toward forgiving those who have harmed us.

Step 1: Agree with God's desire for your life. Without a heart desire to live in agreement with God, there can be no real forgiveness. Do we believe He knows best? Is the Bible inerrant, void of mistakes? Many Scriptures speak about forgiveness, so we know it is an important topic to God. Take a few moments to settle your heart before God. Ask His forgiveness for your wrongs. We are not in agreement with God while we harbor anger or resentment. Who do we want to agree with? Let it be God.

It is natural to want to see our perpetrators suffer like we did, but God calls us to put away our right to see them suffer consequences (John 8:7). If laws have been broken, move forward with the legalities. I have sat in courtrooms, watching as someone receives a deserved life sentence. Release your heart's need for them to suffer. Peace and sweetness are found when we agree with our heavenly Father. Stand in agreement with your God, who wants your heart cleansed of unforgiveness from the poisonous pit where it is entangled. Recognize Satan's role in wanting you shackled to bitterness.

Step 2: If you have not yet completed your list of *who* did *what* to you, do so soon. Remember to write it on a separate sheet of paper. Write the person's name, what they did, and, in a few words, the damage caused by the event. Now, cut each damage done to your heart and mind into a slip of paper. One of my past mentees created her list on toilet paper, one item per square. She is brilliant; how appropriate. I still laugh. I will soon provide examples of my list so you can see what this might look like.

You'll see in the following pages, my forgiveness process that was executed after David and I married the third time. I've repeated some things to allow this to be a stand-alone chapter. I want it to be a ready resource for you, as it may help give insight into how best to complete your list. I pray it benefits you as you change the trajectory of your life.

If you have lost a beloved person or pet, you know what it is to grieve a loss. Perhaps you've cried while watching a movie because the loss of a character tugged at you. We are about to enter a grieving period as we shed the chains of wounds and regrets. Tissues are required, trust me.

> Blessed are those whose lawless deeds
> are forgiven, and whose sins are covered;
> blessed is the man against whom the
> Lord will not count his sin.
> (Romans 4:7–8)

The Forgiveness Process

How to follow the structure of this plan:

1. **The offender (person or group) is in bold,** followed by my perception and thoughts surrounding the offense.

2. *The damage of their actions is italicized.* What I needed to forgive was the result of their actions. I found this to be more meaningful to the condition of my heart than to forgive the offense. As you read the result, think about the damage you need to forgive. Modify your list. Note how the damage formed your decisions in life and how those decisions created more damage. Each damage needs its own slip of paper. Just write a few words for each one, then cut them into slips. I'll number my slips with my mother and father as an example. I had seven slips for my dad.

DENISE RENKEN

My First Ten Years

My mother: From my child's mind, she failed to protect me.
Result: The lack of rescue made me feel vulnerable to the world.
Slip of paper: 1. Feelings of vulnerability

My father: God showed me we all fail and disappoint. Anyone, without God, will fail those around them in terrible ways. Reset of expectations example: With alcohol and heroin, loving responsible decisions remained out of his scope.
Result: I felt vulnerable, with a need to build walls of protection. I feared abandonment, felt unlovable, and feared conflict. My trust was damaged, and I developed a lack of respect for authority.
Slips of paper: 1. Vulnerable 2. Walls 3. Abandonment 4. Unlovable 5. Fear of conflict 6. Damaged trust 7. Lacked respect for authority

My uncle: Sexual abuse. Molested me on two separate occasions. First at age nine, the second at age twelve. Deacon in his church, my mother's brother.
Result: Warped view of relationships, lack of trust, only an object to be used, defenseless, angry, skewed view of church and religion.

Marvin (Linda's husband): Marvin was the guy everyone liked. Smiles, gentle, kind, and thoughtful. He should have protected me. He knew what she was doing. At thirteen, I told Marvin what was happening in the home when he wasn't around. He let me finish and then said, "I know." I asked why he did nothing; he replied, "I do not want to upset her."

Result: Hopeless, only useful as a source of money and Linda's slave, more walls needed, fed my anger, a sense of no value.

Linda: Evil and mentally ill. Nothing else explains her behavior.

Result: I was unlovable, beaten down, frightened, depressed, hopeless, more walls needed, angry, caged (desperate for escape), ugly, had body image issues, judged by her and therefore by the world, lack of trust, rebellious, lack of my own identity, depression, suicide viewed as my only way to escape.

Ages 11—20

First husband: Bullied me, abused me sexually, humiliated me in front of people, lazy, irresponsible, abandoned me to homelessness.

Result: I felt less than enough, a sexual object, a meal ticket, anger, lack of trust, more walls needed, unworthy of kindness or love, fearful, and demoralized.

Everyone associated with me selling myself: This required effort to dissect them all.

Result: Shame, humiliation, bullied, unworthy of real relationships, rebellious, controlled, angry.

Me: For selling myself, the abortion, my rebellion toward God, promiscuity, harmful words toward others. If I believed God forgave me, and I did, then I stood in disagreement with God to not let go of the shame and guilt. I do not understand God's level of love, mercy, forgiveness, and power but I believe it.

Result: Shame, anger, depression, lack of trust in my judgment to make decisions, resigned that I was "less than," self-hatred, controlling, massive walls to keep others out of my life.

The person who raped me:

Result: Victim, more walls needed, lack of trust, fear, anger, numbness to emotional issues, compartmentalization as a coping mechanism, could not trust my discernment of others and what was best for me.

Ages 21—30

Me: Failure to seek God's counsel, struggle for control within the marriage, judging others, gossip, envy of other marriages and possessions, lack of patience with my kiddos.

Result: I grieved the Holy Spirit and my soul. My rage was forced to stay at bay (rather than biblically released). My disobedience to God opened doors for Satan to use the above behavior. All this led to additional stress and a lack of self-respect. Envy led to discontent, and lack of patience led to self-loathing as a mother.

Family: Unbiblical counsel (ranged from not biblical to legalistic), judged, gossiped.

Result: I cared more about what people thought than God's view. This led to continued poor decisions and more self-loathing.

Lady from church who begged me not to remarry David:
Result: Confusion about how to recognize godly counsel.

Ages 31—40

PTA ladies: slanderous, gossiped about me.
Result: I felt judged, isolated, and rejected.

Ages 41—50

David: I've included an overlap of prior years. His adultery, failure to parent (guide), domination, control, micro-manager, broken trust, lying, selfishness, manipulation, and emotional abandonment.

Result: Hopeless, rejected, body image issue, not attractive, lack of trust, felt I was in the way of what he perceived as his perfect life, unworthy of love and kindness, taken for granted, controlled/manipulated, fear, desperate for security, fueled self-reliance rather than reliance on God, depression.

Me: Supporting David's behavior rather than establishing boundaries early in the marriage (codependent), continued intimacy of our relationship (*I felt as if I prostituted myself again*), my disrespectful tone toward David (I continue to struggle), lack of respect shown to David, for all the many ways I failed my children. For making them my god. For my sexual fantasies about other men (*gave Satan a stronghold*).

God knows the sins of the heart and mind. My journey with God began at age thirty-one.

> But I say to you that everyone who looks at
> a woman with lustful intent has already
> committed adultery with her in his heart.
> (Matthew 5:28)

All the *other* women: When I resist God's plan, I verbally argue. We are called to "pray for our enemies." I told God, "I know I'm supposed to do this, and so I will. But I don't mean a word of it." Within a few weeks of obedience in prayer, I wept for these women and their state before the throne of God. Isn't God patient with us? To not want them restored to God was wanting them in hell for eternity. That's a long time. I hope they each come to know Jesus.

What to do with all those slips of paper? How do we approach a deep level of forgiveness for a lifetime of hurts? I'll share how God catapulted me over the last hurdle.

I listen to Christian radio in the car. One day, during an interview, they discussed forgiveness. The interviewee's processes for forgiveness involved the structure of an altar. Yes, an Old Testament stone altar. She instructed listeners to write down what they needed to forgive. Her guidance on what to forgive spoke of the event. I believe stopping at the event without looking at the damage does not result in a complete soul cleansing. The next step included burning them on the altar in a ceremonial release of burdens to God.

Sounded simple enough. The state park was an hour's drive. I decided to write my plethora of grievances on sheets of paper, then tear them into individual strips. No problem.

After some thought, I grew concerned. By the time I dropped the kids off at school, went to the state park, built the altar, and completed the process, I would be on the evening news as the crazy lady who started a forest fire. Plan B was required.

I began with David. I needed to forgive him for not being the husband and father he should have been, for destroying the remnant of trust I still had before marrying him—my self-worth was at zero, for the abandonment I felt, the rejection imprinted on my heart, and more. I began with him because his offenses were the most plaguing. There was no urgency to go through my entire life in one setting. The others came later. It took a month of tears to prepare the David list.

The day arrived to build my altar. With papers in hand, I lit the fireplace and sat cross-legged on the floor. I read the first snippet of paper aloud, shared my broken heart's feelings, and grieved over it. We're talking serious weeping and groaning. I released the sorrow of damage to my heart. I wept because my children did not have the father I wanted for them. I bawled because they lost the childhood I had hoped for them. It didn't mean David would be a terrible dad in the future. But thousands of unretrievable moments of opportunity had passed.

When my well of tears ran dry from the damage on the first slip of paper, I placed it on the altar and prayed, "Dear God, please carry this wound for me. I will no longer give it a place in my heart."

Only then did I pick up the next slip to read aloud, grieve the loss, and give to God. I grieved the loss of trust and how it had impacted my life. I wept for the belief implanted deep into my soul that I was not good enough. It took most of the day to release, forgive, and thank God. His shoulders are much broader than ours.

I'm sure my swollen face was frightful when I picked up the kids from school. No comments came from the back seat. Over the months, I repeated the process for everyone and everything in my life. My soul was breaking free.

Triage Prayer

Father, it is hard to step into forgiveness. The volume and severity of our wounds leave a trail of scars. We can become overwhelmed with the idea of forgiveness. Help clear the dark clouds Satan has created above us. Unshackle the chains of unforgiveness so we can run into Your arms of peace. Heal our wounds but leave a scar as a reminder to avoid that path.

In Jesus's name, Amen

Chapter 13
Molded by the Master's Hands

David and I share our marriage testimony at churches nationwide. Afterward, ladies always come to me in tears, asking the same questions that spurred the writing of this book:

- Why remarry him?

- How did you forgive David?

- How did you restore trust?

This is my quest for trust.

God, The Master, worked in the hearts, souls, and minds of two selfish people to redeem them. Humbled from our arrogance, we knelt before God, begging for marital direction. God took a marriage wrought with decay and raised it from the dead.

Before we remarried, I shared with David the emptiness of my heart. God continued to lay His hands on my mind and soul. Emotionally, I was not a whole woman. What I asked of David was not intended as punishment. I needed time. My request was for us to begin our marriage with an in-house separation. I was determined that this marriage would be void of deceit. If I had given my body to David at that time, I would have felt used. We needed honesty from both sides.

How much time did I need before we consummated the marriage? I didn't share my timing goals with David. The fear of stepping into conflict still ruled. It is worth stressing again that our two primary issues were conflict resolution and communication.

To approach marriage with a separation is different. Open-ended separations are not biblical. For example, to separate with a "let's see how things go" attitude is not God's plan. A structured separation sets a time goal. During this time, both people are actively aligning their hearts with the Lord and seeking counsel from His people. Counsel can be your small church group, a seasoned couple, pastoral support, marriage programs, or a professional Christian counselor. Separation should not reflect selfishness and anger.

It may be an in-house or out-of-house time away. Where possible, an in-house separation is preferred, although not always possible. Set appropriate boundaries to avoid conflict and misunderstandings. Each couple's boundaries will be different. Our agreement eliminated all physical contact. We had meals together and went out together, but we slept in separate bedrooms.

My unspoken plan, via prayer, projected six months for complete restoration. Six months may seem excessive for some or not enough for others. Each couple should assess their needs. Notice, this was an unspoken plan. I did not share it with David. It was not withheld for secrecy; I just lacked the skill to have a detailed conversation about it.

While God provided the gift of my soul realignment throughout the years, I still faced the recent betrayals that culminated in the divorce. I knew the process required for growth and repair, and I knew it would take as long as it would take. My advice is to develop the timing of reconciliation before the separation.

Reflection

Father, thank You for honoring my efforts to seek Your will. I know that we can each discover Your will for our lives by reading Your Word and praying.

> *Do not deprive one another, except perhaps*
> *by agreement for a limited time, that you*
> *may devote yourselves to prayer; but then*
> *come together again, so that Satan may tempt*
> *you because of your lack of self-control.*
> *(1 Corinthians 7:5)*

God's Word tells us we may separate for a time. I did not put a time limit on God. I put a time limit on myself. We married, and David moved upstairs. I prayed and wept daily. My tears did not indicate sorrow. I wept in submission and humility before the throne. I prayed, "Please, God, make me a better daughter to you. Continue to work on David's heart."

I cleansed my home by opening my Bible and reading Scripture from room to room. I demanded any forces of Satan to get out. They had no place in our home. "Father, cleanse David's workplace, my kiddos' schools, and their cars of evil forces." Was this exact process necessary? I'm not sure, but I felt the power of the Holy Spirit in those moments. It connected me to the strength He gives us. "I will fear no evil" (Psalm 23:4). Is there anything scarier than a mama bear protecting her home? I was fierce.

After two months, at my invitation, David moved into our bed. This was my offer: "I want to invite you back to our bed, but I'm not yet ready for intimacy. I'm not angry, just not ready. If moving to the bed will put undue stress on you, we can wait." He moved back into our bedroom. Two months after his move, a surprise for both of us, intimacy was restored.

The deep damage to my life required the continued hand of God. There were times when something triggered old feelings. Did I manage those moments well? Sometimes. Full restoration of a relationship takes a commitment. God's design for marriage became our desire. Divorce was off the table as an option. Rather than just checking a box, we eagerly attended church. We worshipped the God who never abandoned us. Restoration was taking place.

We sought help from our pastor before divorce number two. His counsel was about what he thought rather than what God said about marriage. Just so you know, all advice should be verifiable through Scripture. When we remarried, we returned to seek guidance for the next steps. He offered little hope and seemed eager for us to leave his office. We were on our own.

We bought several couple's devotionals. These spurred what began as our Saturday morning discussion time. Written primarily for newly married couples, they provided some benefits. The Scripture passages presented in the devotion helped. Despite our feeble successes, we remained committed to finding the best path for our marriage using biblical principles.

As our walk with God took ground, so did the marriage. We sought individual heart changes with God, independent of the marriage. If our lives were strong in God, our marriage would follow suit.

A few years into this process, we received a phone call from our youngest. When our kids are happy with us, we are Mom and Dad. When they are less than pleased, we are "You People." Here's how the call went. Our youngest calls me: "My church is starting a three-sermon series on marriage next week. You People wanna come?" Me: "Not sure; let's ask your dad." The phone passes to David. "My church is starting a three-sermon series on marriage. You People need to come." I still laugh.

On Sunday, we were at Watermark Community Church in Dallas (WM). Todd Wagner began his sermon series. The church furnished an online assessment of marriage. We eagerly took advantage of the resource. It was extremely helpful. Seven years into the new marriage, it verified our primary struggles continued to be communication and conflict resolution. Although not a surprise, it was useful to get an official confirmation. We scored well in finances, extended family (put your spouse first), sex, and parenting (we agreed on how to parent). Each category provided a more thorough breakdown for discussion.

We took all this information to use as our Saturday morning discussion tool. We soon realized these Saturday morning discussions needed to vary each week between what we did poorly and what we did well. Otherwise, we felt emotionally beaten by the areas of struggle.

We began regular attendance at Watermark, drawn by the transparency and authenticity we found there. WM was preparing to launch its homegrown re|engage ministry for marriages. Seeking church membership, we met with WM staff to see where we could best be utilized in service. Thoughts of placement in a basement filing paperwork, never to be seen again, crossed my mind. The WM staff person didn't seem shocked as he listened to our marriage woes. He spoke of the upcoming launch of re|engage and suggested we lead a small group. We sat stunned, resembling deer in headlights. David came to his senses first. "I think we should first go through the program." We knew what *not* to do but wanted to know what *to* do. He explained, "Before we help others, we need to address areas in our recovery." They understood our hesitation and did not press us. (For more information about the re|engage marriage ministry, visit www.reengage.org.)

The night re|engage launched, we were in attendance. Beforehand, we had discussed what we planned to share with the group. Fearful of other couples' rejection, we planned to scratch the surface of our past. We didn't know those people and had no plans of spilling our lives out to a group of strangers.

The evening came. We sang worship songs and were dismissed to form small groups of people. I stood for a moment outside the room, thinking, *God, what have I gotten myself into now?* The Holy Spirit pressed into my heart, "You don't need to trust people and what they might say about you. You only need to trust I can carry you through any fire." I opened the door to our small group of folks, and we took seats in a circle. There were four other couples and our facilitating couple.

When re|engage first began, the timeline to complete a small group was about seven months. Today, it runs for four months. It is not a twelve-step program; it's God's plan for marriage, pointing to oneness.

God chose us our facilitators. Wrinkles testified to the trials of their seventy-plus years. Both carried a few extra pounds and smiles which lit the room. They were perfect, and we came to love them.

Our facilitator made eye contact and asked me to start. "What brought you here?" I glanced at David, terrified. God bless him, he said, "Tell them everything." During our first four weekly meetings, I spilled the twenty-plus years of marriage chaos into the room. Astonishingly, no one ran out. They thanked us. It made their stories less difficult and easier to share.

Our facilitators suggested, "When y'all finish this program, you should become leaders." Feeling unworthy and a little afraid of the responsibility, we promised to consider it. Six weeks into the program, we got a call at home from them. "We're on our way to Missouri. We spoke with the WM folks, and they agreed it's okay for y'all to take charge of the meeting tonight. See you next week." We had been tossed into the deep end of the pool. To our amazement, all went well.

After completing the program, we went on to facilitate many small groups. Leading groups through re|engage added strength to our marriage.

Reflection

If we wait until we become perfect, we will never serve. Please throw yourself into the pool where God wants you to serve.

> *Show hospitality to one another without grumbling.*
> *As each has received a gift, use it to serve one another, as*
> *good stewards of God's varied grace: whoever speaks,*
> *as one who speaks oracles of God; whoever serves,*
> *as one who serves by the strength that God supplies—*
> *in order that in everything God may be glorified*
> *through Jesus Christ. To him belong glory and*
> *dominion forever and ever. Amen.*
> *(1 Peter 4:9–11)*

Our communication and conflict-resolution skills significantly improved. One of my favorite pastors once said, "We are either moving forward in our walk with God or moving backward to our sinful nature. There is no such thing as coasting." I sometimes remind myself of this so that my walk does not move in the direction of dormancy.

Steps Toward Trust

1. I *knew* the Holy Spirit urged me back into the marriage. I had His assurance for the future of our marriage. There were limited reasons to trust David, but I knew I could trust God. Boundaries were in place as I let God adjust my heart and watch as He continued to change David. I leaned into the faith of Abraham:

He did not weaken in faith when he considered his own body, which was as good as dead (since he was about a hundred years old), or when he considered the barrenness of Sarah's womb. No unbelief made him waver concerning the promise of God, but he grew strong in his faith as he gave glory to God, fully convinced that God was able to do what he had promised. That is why his faith was "counted to him as righteousness." But the words "it was counted to him" were not written for his sake alone, but for ours also.

It will be counted to us who believe in him who raised from the dead Jesus our Lord, who was delivered up for our trespasses and raised for our justification.
(Romans 4:19–25)

2. David's dedication to God and His Word was evident; it could not be denied. David had a passion for God.

3. David made his life transparent to me. He shared his password for email and began to communicate his feelings and struggles. I did not enjoy listening to his sexual struggles.

Although his sharing was initially important, using me as a long-term accountability partner would be destructive. I did not need to know every time a woman caught his eye. I knew his plan for managing his issues. But, should a temptation arise, he would need to share that with trusted men, just as I share my issues with trusted women. I am not his Holy Spirit. My job is not to identify his sin and convict him to change. I see how he presses into God for direction in small and big decisions. I'm not suggesting we do not counsel one another. But any sexual temptations are for him and the other men, just as he guides the other men with their lustful thoughts.

4. David never pushed or rushed me to the full recovery of the marriage. He respected the time needed for my heart to ready itself. He wanted the best for me, not just himself.

5. David's daily demeanor reflected a shift in his heart and head. He was dedicated to the success of his family and willing to accept his part in the destruction of it.

6. He was *consistent* with the dedication to spiritual growth beyond the ground taken.

7. He knew it was not my job to hold him accountable. Accountability was God's job and David's job. Accountability now includes a close group of men.

8. The evidence of real change in David's life was clear. God alone creates full restoration. Trusting God was my everything and still is today. Otherwise, I could not have penned this book. The above list, and the restoration of two hearts, granted me trust in David and the future of our marriage. It has been over twenty years since we remarried. Thank You, Father, for blessing our efforts toward obedience. Not once have I seen signs of regression.

Triage Prayer

Lord, broken trust can damage our trust in You and other people. We lose our ability to trust our judgment to make sound decisions. Father, clear the fog and allow us to see clearly who to trust and who to wait on. Protect our hearts.

In Jesus's name, Amen

Chapter 14
A Note from David

Denise asked me to write a few words about my life change. She was reluctant to ask, even after twenty-plus years of my surrendering control to God. It is a reminder to me that parts of her are still wounded. These are visible signs of the sin I brought into the marriage.

Through much prayer and leaning into God, the fear of failure has gone. The flesh, our natural man instincts, seeks to return me to a state where I accept the chains He has broken. Proverbs 26:11 succinctly states, "Like a dog that returns to his vomit is a fool who repeats his folly."

Early in life, I learned that love or attention was transactional; you needed to give people what they wanted. Most often, this manifests itself in *people-pleasing*, but that wasn't what drove me. It may have started that way, but very soon, it developed into a way to manipulate others. Be it a parent, teacher, or female acquaintance, all seemed to respond to the same approach. I do not know exactly when I developed this cynical approach to relationships and *love,* but I honed it over the years.

I accepted Christ at age eight at a Salvation Army vacation Bible school. For the first time, I was exposed to the love of Christ. My parents had taken us to a different church but stopped attending. God seemed violent and angry—*fire and brimstone*. The Salvation Army message, shared by Commandant Homer Horton, spoke of Christ's unconditional (agape) love for all. The Holy Spirit led me to the front of the worship center, where I confessed my childhood sins and accepted Christ. However, since positive reinforcement from home was not given, I quickly succumbed to peer pressure and no longer attended church.

I took pride in my grades and was considered a model student. I knew what others wanted to see. Inside, I was full of insecurity, doubts, and a feeling of being *less than* others. My unwritten mantra became, "If you do not feel, you can't be hurt."

My folks provided a home but failed to model a good marriage. Homelife included episodes of violent outbursts (directed at us children), exposure to excessive alcohol, and sexual abuse from an older cousin and brother. Shame kept me from sharing these offenses with anyone until adulthood.

Full-time work began at age fifteen, after school and on weekends. I believed anything worthwhile in life depended on me. The job introduced me to much older guys, which accelerated my damaging habits.

None of this background is meant to excuse my later choices or elicit empathy. It explains some of the reasons I questioned myself. At seventeen, God intervened on my first path of destruction. My attempt to use recreational drugs gave way to a churning stomach. "God, please get me through this." My one-time drug party ended.

In my family, sex was not discussed. My dad broached the subject when I was fifteen. I stopped him, saying, " It's too late." He questioned me further. "I haven't done anything yet. I've seen the impact of starting a family early or without planning." He became angry and called me a liar. I didn't argue. How he viewed me did not matter. By age sixteen, I had crossed the sexual boundary. Neither of us was ready for commitment. Within a few weeks, she broke my heart.

I had a few more girlfriends in high school but emotionally distanced them. If they wanted a true relationship, I would deliberately anger them. It forced them to break up with me. This was my pattern.

I took the ACT, received an academic scholarship, and attended university. My job was going well, and school was fun, but I soon became bored. The hole in my heart still existed, and I was unwilling to put effort into repair.

I met a young woman at work and asked her to marry me in two months. The relationship was fueled by distrust and infidelity by both parties. This marriage was chock-full of separation and infidelity and did nothing for either of us beyond a wasted three years. Added to the dysfunction was debt. What a mess. Agreeing that divorce was the best solution, I gave her our savings, leaving me enough to pay a month's rent. Once again, my actions succeeded in pushing her to make the decision.

Earning money was never an issue for me. I worked full-time at Texas Instruments, attended community college in the evenings, and added two part-time jobs on the weekends. It was at Texas Instruments that I first saw Denise. There was something different about her beyond the fact that she was aloof. It took me three or four weeks to get a date with her, but I persevered. My thoughts at the time were that she was beautiful and worked hard. She had two full-time jobs, wanted more from life, and was prepared to start college part-time. I still remember what she wore on our first date, where we went, and much of the conversation.

No steps had been taken to address my character issues or my thoughts on relationships. Relationships were supposed to make you happy, weren't they? I had not welcomed God back into my life. I began asking Denise to marry me the first week. Deep down, I did not see how she might want to marry me as my self-worth issues ran deep. The urgency? If she knew me, I would not stand a chance. Surprisingly, she accepted after my fourth time asking.

We quickly adjusted to married life. Jobs and school kept us busy. The little time we spent with each other was all quality time. I fought back jealousy issues, not understanding they were self-created. Deep down, I believed it was just a matter of time before someone better came into her life. In the first year, we became pregnant. We downsized employment to one job each and continued college. I participated in baby planning but began to feel a loss of her undivided attention. Twenty-one months after our first baby's birth, our second was born.

I began to seek other women's attention at work and school. I loved Denise and our children but did not know how to show love to anyone except myself. The wall around my feelings had never come down. Denise had been able to poke a few holes in it, but my warped views on relationships remained.

The first affair was the culmination of months of conversations at work and the timing of her spouse walking out. I was the *friend* with whom she shared private issues. I thought, *What would it hurt?*

It was not something long-term, and no one need know. It stroked my ego. If Denise and I did not make it long-term, my life would not be one bereft of companionship. Why was I so afraid of being alone?

This started the cycle of affairs that became the norm in our lives. I knew it was wrong but did not have the strength of character to stop. The excitement of a new conquest, someone wanting me beyond my wife, was too big of a lure. Affairs served as an escape from the stress of our day-to-day life.

Denise may have suspected, but until the pattern was well established in our marriage, she did not confront me with the evidence. I graduated from night college with a degree in accounting, passed the CPA exam, and accepted a new, much higher-paying job in high-tech. The position wanted someone with an MBA. I was glib and closed the deal, "I'm starting on mine soon." I began attending Southern Methodist University's (SMU's) three-year evening MBA program.

Soon after starting my MBA, Denise confronted me with evidence of the most recent affair. I swore I would break it off but never did. Taking matters into her own hands, she met with the other woman to plead her case. The other woman called to tell me what happened. Rather than seeing a wife who loved her husband and was willing to do anything to save the marriage, I was concerned about how the other woman would see me. Within a few days, I moved out. After all, I thought Denise would be better off without me. I do not recall having much thought about the impact on our children.

That affair, like all the others, soon faded. I sat in a small apartment with rented furniture and a twelve-inch black-and-white TV. I opened my childhood Bible and read passages. I missed my wife and children. I saw how much better life was before I moved out of our home. Work was still going fine. I had learned to compartmentalize my life and was able to shut out any other distractions.

After five months, Denise accepted me back. My issues were unaddressed, and I had not sought counseling. I appeased Denise by attending church, but I wasn't ready for what God offered. After six months, I stopped going to church. My reasoning was, "My MBA studies and work demands consume my Sundays and any spare time."

I graduated with my MBA and accepted a transfer to North Carolina. The transfer came with a promotion and the gain of work experience. Nothing changed. Within a month, I had a new interest. I would juggle multiple affairs in varying degrees as one fell away or got too close. I realized no one else would make me happy, as the newness with anyone soon wore off. I loved Denise and the kids but ignored the effects of my actions on them. Selfish.

I was not a total loss during those years. I coached our kids' sports teams and attended school plays and musicals. I believed these activities made me a good father but a lousy husband. The way I failed our kids fills me with regret to this day. After five years in North Carolina, I needed to transfer somewhere to further my career. Denise's grandparents were aging and in poor health, so I requested a move back to Dallas.

For a while, I did well in my strength. The move to Dallas kept me busy, but I found time to groom my next affair. Denise continued to plug away at college and found a renewed focus on her spiritual life, which had begun in Raleigh. I encouraged both. I felt sorry for the life I had given Denise. Over the years, she had not given me any reason to doubt her sincerity when she said our vows.

What was it? How can someone say they love you and do what I did? I look back and wonder at my stupidity. So many years chasing after what I thought would make me happy and feel valued. God had given me all I needed (in Him) and provided a family I could not dare dream of.

Denise continued to pray for and over me for two decades. Looking back, I see that only God's strength gave her the ability to persevere.

We had separated during the Thanksgiving 2000 holiday. The Friday after, I was at the house to help decorate for Christmas and visit our kids. Two weeks earlier, I had ended my most recent affair and was pursuing Denise at the house. The doorbell rang.

Denise answered, and my heart sank. I felt my stomach rise to my mouth; it was her. She told Denise, "David left some of his things at my apartment," as she handed Denise the bag. Seconds seemed an eternity. I thought Denise was going to pass out before the encounter ended. Denise robotically took the bag, watched her walk away, and closed the door. Then the tears came as Denise told me, "Leave, never come back." In a moment, I saw what my actions had done to her. Hopelessness replaced the joy of moments before. I understood the insufficiency of my words in changing anything.

During the short drive to my apartment, the full significance began to dawn on me. My selfish actions had just taken away everything that mattered to me. The picture of her utter hopelessness was etched in my mind as I asked myself why. Why was I pursuing others? Why wasn't anything ever enough and what was missing in me? My thoughts began to turn to suicide.

The depth of my actions fell on me. The scales over my eyes for all those years were torn off as I crumbled to the floor. I cried out to God, begging Him to take control; my running of the family had destroyed all I held dear. I lost my wife, my kids, and my self-respect (if ever I had any). "God, I'm tired of hurting those I love." I found myself on my knees, a state I had not been in since accepting Christ as an eight-year-old boy at the Salvation Army church.

My thoughts cleared, and a weight lifted from my shoulders—the weight of the unrepentant sin of a lifetime. I burned all the notes and phone numbers of women. I closed the six personal email accounts. I was through; I had come to the end. In the past, I would feign change: *I will just set these aside and never use them.*

After the purging, I fell asleep. The next morning, with the huge weight removed, I wanted to call someone. I had no one to call. My life was nothing more than an actor in a play. The only person who knew me did not want to see me again, and who could blame her? I prayed for God to show me the next steps. I picked up my Bible and spent the rest of the weekend getting reacquainted with God, the same God I had walked away from years before.

Monday morning, the mess made of my life and my family's lives struck me anew. God had forgiven me, but looking at the destruction I brought was horrifying. I called Denise to let her know everything would be okay. God was in charge. She barely answered, when my hello was met with the phone slamming in my ear, as she said, "Never call me." For a moment, old narcissism kicked in, and I was upset. Didn't she know God had changed me?

I made a God-directed call to an associate pastor at a local church. Pouring out my story to him, I expected sympathy when he said, "You sinned against God and your family. Your life with Denise may be over, but know God is not through with you." We prayed for me to be the best single godly man possible and ended the conversation with an invitation to his church's men's Bible study.

In the past, I would have sought another woman to make me feel better or maybe even gone back to a previous affair partner where my words would still be welcomed. I would blame all of our marriage woes on Denise. This time was different. I did not need someone to make me feel better about myself. I understood I was a sinner in need of a Savior, and only through His strength would I ever have a meaningful life. Philippians 4:13 says, "I can do all things through him who strengthens me." Grateful for the crushing weight of sin He took, I never wanted it on my back again.

I attended the Sunday services and the men's Bible study on Fridays. Denise followed through on a divorce. How could I blame her? I had given her two decades of misery, and my actions robbed her of the hope of change. My days were filled with work, physical workouts, and my Bible. I began to understand the peace in knowing I was in God's will for my life.

I found a good Christian psychologist to help with my deeply embedded issues. With his help, daily prayer, and time with God, I began to understand how flawed my thinking had been. My heavenly Father, God, truly did love me.

The men's Bible study provided a vehicle to share what was going on in my life. Before I completed the six-week session, I stood in front of the sixty men in the room and shared my sin, what I had done in our marriage.

At the men's group, I first heard the acronym RALE—a man needs to **R**eject passivity, **A**ccept responsibility, **L**ead courageously, and **E**xpect the greater reward. The guys at my table continued to meet every other week to discuss our successes and failures, which was my first introduction to the Christian community.

Many of the concepts presented were new to me. I created a plan to read my Bible, something I had not done before. God's Word fell on fertile soil. I accepted responsibility for my sin, not blaming it on my childhood, parents, friends, and most importantly, Denise. It was abundantly clear to me that the one constant in my struggles throughout life was me. I realized God forgave my sin as I repented, but the consequences would be with me.

I read the Bible in four months. I did not sleep well and read at whatever time I happened to wake up. I began to see how God's Word directly applied to my life—His intention for me to live abundantly. I wanted to model King David's story. He owned his sin, confessed, repented, and dealt with the consequences. I sent Denise emails, not knowing if she ever read them. I explained what I was reading, how it impacted my heart, and what actions I was taking in my life.

Denise finalized our divorce in early 2001, our second divorce. Disheartened, I did not blame her for going through with it. My decades of deceit might be forgiven, but to dream of restoration was a bridge too far. I consciously did not think of it. In my dreams, I was living it. I understood I would be married to Denise in God's eyes despite the divorce. Now I needed to live a godly single life. Some in my family told me to move on, but I knew that was not His plan. I told folks I still loved her; we were not together due to my actions, not hers; I had chosen the path. Months went by. I occasionally saw her on Saturday mornings.

One Sunday morning, after service at church, I received a call. Denise asked if I wanted to join her at the Dallas Opera for a Sunday matinee. Her friend had canceled at the last minute. In two seconds, I said yes despite the event—the opera. We ended up leaving at the first intermission. We talked at length. It was the first time we had spoken for more than a few minutes in a long time.

I told myself, "Don't read anything into the *date*; we're two people who care for each other and are just talking." Over the months, we did find time for lunch or coffee. I did not believe the possibility, but I asked if we might get married again. I decided to let God lead the family. I expected a resounding no, thinking she could not, or would not, put herself in that position again. She said she would think and pray. I understood. A few weeks later, she said yes.

What was different when we married the third time?

1. I made Christ the cornerstone of our marriage.

2. I prayed:
   For God's direction for our lives.
   For Him to help me/us to love each other well.

3. I stayed in His Word.

4. We found a church where we could serve as a couple and have community.

5. I made our marriage a priority.

6. We properly addressed conflict.

7. We stopped wounding each other with words (communication).

Still a work in progress, God has allowed us to share His redemption of our marriage with thousands through our testimony. Looking back, I do not recognize the man I was, but I realize the events remain a part of me. I look at the years wasted with regret. I remember what John Piper said regarding the compost piles in life: "Don't pitch a tent."[16] It is okay to look back, but realize it is the past.

The voice in my ear that said "You will never change" has been silenced by God's words in Romans 8:1: "There is therefore now no condemnation for those who are in Christ Jesus." God has given us this day, and I plan to live it to the fullest.

Chapter 15
Conflict Resolution

Our wounded hearts were healing. Now the time had come to deal with our inability to resolve conflict. After studying various techniques, David and I created a unique plan. Sitting at the kitchen table, coffee in hand, the Renken Rules launched into action. We have used these conflict-resolution rules with other relationships. Although one-sided, we have witnessed how they deescalate conflict and provide a godly view of resolution with others.

The Renken Rules of Engagement

The Rules go into effect at the first sign of conflict. This might be a look, tone of voice, or words. It is any sign of potential agitation, subjective to whichever spouse feels it. Here are the rules we agreed to:

1. **No storming out of the room.** While our struggle did not include storming out of the house, calling names, or throwing things, it is important to leave nothing to miscommunication. Permission was granted for a *peaceful* withdrawal.

   a. Gently signal to the other person that you need a timeout. We used the same hand signal used for a timeout in sports. I recommend a nonverbal cue because your tone of voice during conflict may not be at its best.

   b. During your timeout, there is to be no TV, games, or social media—nothing except you, the Bible, and God (for both people). This allows hearts to settle into a godly posture. You're asking God to take control of your attitude. Are you trying to get your way? Is it important you prove you are right? Or are you aligned with God's heart?

   c. When one of you is ready (the heart is God-centered), you let the other person know you are ready to continue the discussion. If the other person is not ready, wait with patience. They should let you know when they are ready.

   d. When both of you are ready, step back into the conversation where you left off. If it begins to go poorly again, return to this process, starting with a peaceful withdrawal.

2. **Don't poke the bear.** Deliberately triggering a negative response does not make you the winner. Nothing good will come of clinging to your right to be right. Only God is right. Arguing for the sake of winning does not align with God. If it is not of God, by default, it is Satan-driven.

3. **Louder doesn't make you right.** Raised voices cause us to lose credibility. This applies to your children, too.

4. **Don't assume the worst.** One evening, David came through the door after work. I was in the kitchen finishing dinner. He quickly walked past me. Not a smile, not a "hello" or "dinner smells good." He just hurried past me. My mind raced with thoughts: *He hates what I'm cooking; I must look worse than I thought; I failed to do something he wanted me to do; I did something to annoy him before he left for work.*

   a. Pause your mind to give the other person the benefit of the doubt. In reality, he'd had another cup of coffee on the way home and was uncomfortably racing to the bathroom.

   b. Assume the best of the other person, that their intention is not to cause you harm. David didn't mean to cause a panic; he just really needed to go.

5. **Get your affirmation from God.** We should affirm and encourage each other, but a dependency on supportive comments from other people will disappoint. We go to God to affirm our value; our spouse is a poor version of God.

6. **Don't say things like, "You shouldn't feel that way," "That makes no sense," or "Just get over it."**

    a. If the person believes their views or feelings are minimized, they probably are minimized.

    b. We filter events and information via our history and our current relationship with God. It is common to recall events differently. A different recollection does not make it false.

    c. We need time to heal wounds caused by actions and words. There is no such thing as "getting over it." Only God steps in to repair the harm caused.

7. **Don't say, "I'm sorry." Instead, ask, "Will you forgive me?"** Asking for forgiveness carries the humility God requires and a deeper sincerity.

8. **Don't correct each other in front of people.** Does it matter if something happened on a Tuesday or a Wednesday? Correcting your spouse publicly is disrespectful. When we disrespect our spouse, we disrespect ourselves and God.

9. **Stop talking.** Heed the advice in James 1:19 that tells us, "Know this, my beloved brothers: let every person be quick to hear, slow to speak." We are to consider the other person's perspective. Ask yourself, "Will what I'm about to say bring honor to God?" "Will it be beneficial to my spouse?" If not, stop. Although I haven't mastered this yet, I remain committed to conquering my utterances.

What about the casual remarks, things said in passing? Those things outside of the face-to-face conversations where the Renken Rules don't apply?

Think about how deep, painful bruises take a long time to heal. Those swollen purple bruises tend to linger. I'm sure you've experienced cutting a corner too closely or hitting your thigh on the edge of a table. I once failed to open the car door correctly, and it came back to smack me. Ouch! These bruises are tender, and a mere bump to the area causes additional pain. Without the deep bruise, the bump is just an insignificant annoyance.

As it relates to our topic, some comments we make to our spouse might be a mere bump, but because the comment struck an emotional bruise, it is painful. And just like a deep physical bruise, the impact of the words hinders the recovery of the hurt. Remarks made in passing conversations can cause these bumps, even though they are unintentional. What to do about passing remarks that strike an already bruised heart? Satan's goal is for the bruise to remain. He wants us to be angry and in conflict.

Sometimes we weren't in a face-to-face conversation when these occurred and needed a method to acknowledge the injury. We decided to apply a variation of the Renken rules to cushion the bump's impact. We would leave a sticky note informing the other person of a particular offense on their computer screen (when they are not using the computer, of course). The need for a technical disclaimer is amusing. Don't do this. Don't slap a sticky note in the middle of the screen he's using. Don't use a hair dryer while you're in the shower. Don't eat the bar of soap. Disclaimers are funny.

Placing the sticky note allowed time for the other person to process what he or she had done to warrant the post. A response might be a simple, "Okay, got it," or "I have no idea what you mean, let's talk." Our approach was always with a Christ-centered heart. We wanted God to cure the bruises, and we knew He would honor our hearts. We discussed the intent of what had been said and how to communicate better going forward. We should have bought stock in 3M. I'm sure our purchases of sticky notes helped corporate earnings.

The first six months of our conflict resolution annoyed us. The frequency of use was high, sometimes daily. But our determination to alter our approach to conflict won out. We wanted a marriage, not just a roommate.

The second six months became easier. By year two, the need for withdrawals seldom arose. Our process developed into our automatic reaction to conflict. It took time and diligence, but the reward was worth it.

And by year two, this process had encountered and resolved most of our issues. Deep bruises healed. God taught us how to remain Christ-centered in the struggle. Disputes became a rarer occurrence. Our lifelong preference to avoid conflict continues, but knowing how to process disagreements taught us the benefit of moving into the conflict. When we get to the other side of issues, we are better people, and I can honestly say our marriage is a joy.

Commitment to reading God's Word and serving others also helped with conflict. Service took our minds off petty issues. Believe me when I say His Word changes hearts. I cannot over-emphasize the importance of the Bible. It softens the rough edges, the tongue, and our human perspectives.

Reflection

Thank You, Father, for the work you did in our marriage. You knew the timing for us to seek a different church. It led us to become a part of Watermark Community Church and the re|engage ministry. Thank You for providing the courage needed to share my life story. You alone know the difficulty of penning this book.

The Lord is my helper; I will not fear;
what can man do to me?
(Hebrews 13:6)

Triage Prayer

Father, You know we often move with selfish hearts. We want our way and to win the argument. With heels dug in, determined not to give an inch, chaos bears down. Show us Your way, heart, and desire for our lives as we approach others. Gently massage our pride out of the way. Guide us to set boundaries while moving toward peace.

Whether a marriage, a parent, a child, or a coworker, we want the relationship improved. Adjust our expectations, protect and heal our souls.

In Jesus's name, Amen

Chapter 16
What Satan Meant for Evil, God Uses for Good

Satan stalks his prey, God's creation, seeking ways to devour us. He uses the fallenness of this world—disease, heartaches, and evil people—to lure us away from God. This is why I chose the opening passage for *Triage* from the book of Genesis.

> As for you, you meant evil against me,
> but God meant it for good, to bring it
> about that many people
> should be
> kept alive, as they are today.
> (Genesis 50:20)

Our wounded souls often are fed by the toxic roots nourished by Satan. How do we break free from the shackles of past regrets? How do we bring God to the forefront of our lives to draw His sword on the battlefield of redemption? We need Him to heal our roots. He leaves the flock to find each of us. He loves us.

Professional counseling, church programs, and mentoring offer assistance in healing. I stand with the belief that unless God is the primary healer, we are not healed at a spiritual level. If my spirit is at odds with God, I am at odds with God. First Corinthians 10:31 tells us to do everything for the glory of God. We include Him in the healing process to benefit our mind and soul but also to bring God glory. He gets the credit.

> But we have this treasure in jars of clay, to show that the surpassing power belongs to God and not to us. We are afflicted in every way, but not crushed; perplexed, but not driven to despair; persecuted, but not forsaken; struck down, but not destroyed; always carrying in the body the death of Jesus, so that the life of Jesus may also be manifested in our bodies. For we who live are always being given over to death for Jesus' sake, so that the life of Jesus also may be manifested in our mortal flesh. So death is at work in us, but life in you.
>
> Since we have the same spirit of faith according to what has been written, "I believed, and so I spoke," we also believe, and so we also speak, knowing that he who raised the Lord Jesus will raise us also with Jesus and bring us with you into his presence. For it is all for your sake, so that as grace extends to more and more people it may increase thanksgiving, to the glory of God.
>
> So we do not lose heart. Though our outer self is wasting away, our inner self is being renewed day by day. For this light momentary affliction is preparing for us an eternal weight of glory beyond all comparison,

as we look not to the things that are seen but to the things that are unseen. For the things that are seen are transient, but the things that are unseen are eternal. (2 Corinthians 4:7–18)

As you move toward restoring your mind and soul, I recommend three action steps that have helped me along the way.

Trust. God waits for you to turn to Him. The course we take will not be easy, but the value of the finish line is immeasurable. He will heal you and direct your steps. Trust Him.

Did you know the minute instructions given to Noah to build the ark excluded a rudder? God moved the boat in the direction He chose; Noah was dependent on God. To travel life's journey without God at the rudder of your ship is like having no rudder at all. You will continue to be tossed about at the mercy of the world which cares not for you. Trust God.

Forgive. Forgive others; forgive yourself. Purge your heart of anger, bitterness, and thoughts unaligned with the heart of our Savior Jesus. This is not a simple ask. It is difficult when there have been so many betrayals. The world, which has cursed God, betrays all. Allow the Holy Spirit to cleanse your precious heart. Allow Jesus to cradle you in His arms as He brings you back home to Him. He alone can restore and lead you in how to protect your heart. Remember, condoning and restoration are not required. Forgive.

Pray. Pray for His guidance, for Him to place His people around you, to find a good church, for a desire to read His Word, and how best to serve others. Service can be in small ways until you are ready for bigger tasks. He always, always, always blesses small steps toward obedience. Do these things. I will continue to pray for you. Pray.

This book is written out of my love and compassion for a world of hurting women. You are not alone. The world is in the midst of a mental and spiritual crisis. Please don't separate the two issues. Roots connect our mental and spiritual health. The condition of our roots drives the condition of the fruit, and the fallen fruit then feeds the roots. We must allow God to repair our roots.

Be thorough in your list of damages. I recommend creating your lists before beginning the forgiveness step. Don't rush the process. Healing is not something to check off your to-do list. Savor this time with God. When we rush things, we risk seizing control of the process rather than letting God guide us. If it is not clear which person to forgive first, ask Him. He might want you to start with something easy, just to remove a small wound, before proceeding to bigger issues. God will *triage* your mind and soul and create a restored woman.

Your Sister in Christ,
Denise

Appendix
Finding a Mentor

In 2 Corinthians 1:4, the apostle Paul instructs the believers to comfort others with the comfort we have received. Titus 2:3–4 encourages older women to mentor younger women. My path to healing included eighteen months of therapy with a psychologist, Erikson's analytical tools, and a precious woman who mentored me toward God's solutions. I take these passages to heart, knowing how invaluable a mentor can be in the life of another woman.

What is a mentor? A mentor is someone to walk the healing process with you. We discuss issues, comfort, encourage, pray, dispense tissues, listen, and help you learn to set boundaries. Scripture should back our advice. We are your champion on the battlefield for a better future.

Some of the women I mentor utilize a professional counselor while I serve as a mentor. Others process their issues via a faith-based program while I walk the journey at their side. Or I may guide them through the process without anyone other than God. A mentor can be used with or without a professional counselor or a faith-based program.

Each mentor's process will differ. For me, a lady comes to my home weekly. These visits last about two hours as I allow her to process the issue at the top of her list. I only mentor one lady at a time because it requires my devotion to the journey, lasting about fifteen months. Outside of our visits, we use text messages for other communication needs. I've been known to text short prayers or check on them. When our time together is complete, our frequency of contact transitions to monthly, then quarterly, as I move my focus to the next person. Just as a mama bird nudges the young out, the time always comes for my ladies to leave the nest.

As we navigate their wounds, I direct them to stay on God's path, not the world's vision of right and wrong. My preference follows Erikson's stages. We gently peel back the life layers chronologically, savoring the sweet moments when God stepped in. This is not a quest to assess blame, and I'm not inclined to toss relationships away unless necessary. There may be unavoidable people in need of limitations—family, biblically unsound church folks, and coworkers, to name a few. The proper management of those relationships requires boundaries. We can think of boundaries as triage on the battlefield. We need to find a way to evaluate what injuries take priority for repair, stop the bleeding (boundaries), and bring God into the process.

Many women ask me how they should go about choosing a mentor. This should be a thoughtful, deliberate decision. It helps to know your expectations and communicate those. If possible, get a recommendation from a trusted friend. You need someone who understands how to traverse the deep valleys of life with God's assistance, meaning she should have already processed her life issues with a counselor, faith-based ministry, or Christian mentor. She also should have zero residual anger. Someone spewing her anger will not help you to process yours. Her unprocessed pain will not help you. You desire empathy extended through the voice of God's peace and hope. When I began to seek God's will for my life, my friends consisted of a mixture of toxic anger and folks in various stages of peace and mental recovery. The angry ones needed boundaries.

When you begin your mentoring relationship, it is important to remove any obstacles that get in the way. It can be difficult to remove toxic friends and family who want to be a part of your process. Toxic family members may not embrace your path to peace and may become defensive. Fearing you may share the family junk in discussions with your mentor can generate varied responses.

Toxic friends may shun you as your behavior changes from negative to positive. They may want you to continue joining them as they verbally blast their offender. They will miss you blasting away at your offender and want to drag you back down.

I'm not suggesting you end relationships. As we travel the struggles of life, it may not be the time to make permanent decisions. The caveat is violent behavior. Never remain in a dangerous environment. Seek shelter immediately. Contact a women's shelter for guidance and a plan of exit.

When God began working in my heart, I was surprised by the disappearance of friends and the distancing of some family. I decided to silence the angry voices who served as my comrades in misery. I reduced the frequency of communication with them. I shifted contact to once per month or once per quarter. When I set a firm boundary with toxic friends and family, it went something like this: "I'm so glad to see you and catch up. First, I need to ask a big favor. I won't be discussing the issues between David and me. I'm taking some time to process issues with a professional. I need our time together to be about anything except David." No one was thrilled with this plan. I had to remind a few folks with a gentle, "I'm not comfortable talking about David." Because of my unwillingness to angrily wade through the mud, folks began to disappear from my circle of friends. Their reciprocation of sent Christmas cards halted. I've seen this phenomenon repeated in other women's lives. A trail of rejection by others will follow you as you move toward His peace and joy. Rejection and judgment are hurtful. Not everyone will celebrate your pursuit of peace.

Think of a favorite relative or friend who fits the mentor criteria and ask them to join you as you move toward healing your mind and heart. I will pray for you.

Triage Prayer

Father, rejection is a painful experience. We move toward Your plan, knowing there will be a loss of some folks. It is a difficult step. May others want more of You because of what they see in me.

In Jesus's name, Amen

Notes

1. Erik H. Erikson *Identity: Youth and Crisis* (W. W. Norton Company, 1968), 97.

2. Erikson, *Identity: Youth and Crisis*, 103.

3. Erikson, *Identity: Youth and Crisis*, 108.

4. Erikson, *Identity: Youth and Crisis*, 109.

5. Erikson, *Identity: Youth and Crisis*, 109.

6. Erikson, *Childhood and Society*, 3rd ed. (W. W. Norton Company, 1963), 252.

7. Erikson, *Identity: Youth and Crisis*, 119.

8. Erikson, *Identity: Youth and Crisis*, 122.

9. Erikson, *Identity: Youth and Crisis*, 124.

10. Erikson, *Identity: Youth and Crisis*, 127.

11. Erikson, *Childhood and Society*, 263.

12. Erikson, *Childhood and Society*, 263.

13. Erikson, *Identity: Youth and Crisis*, 135.

14. Erikson, *Identity: Youth and Crisis*, 136.

15. Shawna Seed, "Codependency: Signs and Symptoms," March 1, 2024 webmd.com/mental-health/signs-codependency.

16. John Piper, *This Momentary Marriage: A Parable of Permanence*, reprint edition (Crossway Publishing, 2009), 59.

About the Author

Denise Renken loves to visit other places, but she and her husband, David, call Texas home. Her formal credentials include a CPA and MBA, but her passion is serving women. Her heart is drawn to other women's troubled souls and how best to move them into the capable arms of Jesus. Whether speaking at a women's event or mentoring, as she has done for over thirty-five years, she finds ways to encourage women. She and David have also served in marriage ministry for twenty years; they continue to share their testimony nationwide.

Denise enjoys researching Scripture and how to apply it to her life as a daughter of God. She holds family time as precious, loves animals (especially German shepherds), and treasures her sisters in Christ. No one will ever commission her to write a cookbook. The things that come from her kitchen range from tasty to puzzling. She knows that "finding the humor in life is essential."

Connect with Denise Renken, Christian Author and Speaker

Invite Denise to speak at WomenSpeakers.com

Website: restoredforhim.com

Facebook: https://www.facebook.com/profile.php?id=100009568657790

LinkedIn: https://www.linkedin.com/in/denise-Renken-2a5b40155/s

TRIAGE

ORDER INFORMATION

To order individual copies go to
redemption-press.com/bookstore

For discounts on bulk orders
send an email to
bookorders@redemption-press.com.
subject: bulk orders

www.ingramcontent.com/pod-product-compliance
Lightning Source LLC
Chambersburg PA
CBHW071103080525

26227CB00012B/23